# Through Faith

## An Adoption and Missionary Journey

Stephen St. John

# DEDICATION

To the girl in the picture. For the glory of God.

# CONTENTS

Acknowledgements     1

Introduction     3

1    In Madagascar     7

2    In America     20

3    Learning More About Adoption     26

4    Heartstrings and Heartbreak     33

5    Moving Ahead     41

6    A Surprise Call     47

7    Ngo Thi Xaun Mai     56

8    Dark Days     61

9    In Indonesia     77

10    In Vietnam     93

11    Post Adoption Challenges     110

12    Conclusion (For Now)     120

Bibliography     123

About the Author     124

# ACKNOWLEDGMENTS

God provided so many individuals to aid us along the way that I hesitate to attempt a list of acknowledgments. Nevertheless, there is no question that my family deserves some special mention.

Joshua, Andrew, Jacob, Simon, Elijah, and Grace gave up a bit of themselves while mom and dad adventured around. They did it because they love God, their sister, and us.

Our parents Bob and Susan St. John, Doug and Jamie Sharp, and Dennis Young have shown us love and support far beyond the norm.

Jennifer's sister Jill, my brother Matthew and his wife Christa, along with their daughters Emily and Katy, have gone the extra mile for us again and again.

And then there is my dear Jennifer. Quiet, shy, hesitant at times, but fierce like a lion when it comes to needy children.

## INTRODUCTION

There are risks in writing a book like this. It is a personal story. Some of the details are icky and make us look bad. Why, I sometimes wonder, share those stories? More dangerous, perhaps, are details that might make me look like some sort of admirable person. The truth is, I am not a great person. In fact, I am a man who has let others down, who has sometimes hurt his family members, who struggles with sins, and who wonders daily if I am getting things right. Those who know me best could affirm the truth of that last sentence. However, those may be reasons to write a book like this. God uses ordinary people, even messed up people, to accomplish his goals. If he can use a family like ours, then he can use yours too. Guaranteed!

Although I am the writer, this is not my story. It belongs first to Almighty God, who declared, "pure religion is… to take care of orphans in their affliction" (James 1:27). Secondly, it belongs to a little girl who was dropped abruptly outside the gate of a state-run orphanage, given over by people close to her, but not abandoned by her Father in heaven. Thirdly, it belongs to my wife and children, who prayed, worked, and sacrificed some temporary pleasure so we might experience the lasting joy of a new family member. Finally, it belongs to a host of others who helped with and prayed for our adoption process.

I began writing with four goals in mind. These are still my prayers for the book. First, I pray that God would be glorified by this story. He is the One who gives us strength to do extraordinary things in this world and all people ought to know and see how awesome He is. Second, I pray that readers who are considering adoption will be encouraged to go ahead. The journey can be difficult, but it is worth it. Third, I pray that readers will begin to look beyond the typical "American dream" of temporal comfort and take some risks for the glory of God and the good of the world. The truth is, letting go of "the pursuit of happiness" is the best way to find happiness. Fourth, my prayer is for this book to become a source of funds for future adoptions.

I tried to be as accurate as possible in relating this story. Obviously, some of the narrative dialog had to be constructed purely from memory and therefore is not *exactly* the way it was said. In those cases, I have done my best to communicate the exact meaning of the conversations, if not the exact words.

It is probably worth noting that I am sharing from my perspective. There are important individuals in the narrative who may not have seen it exactly as I did. For example, while I communicate the genuine way our children Joshua, Andrew, Jacob, Simon, Elijah, and Grace supported the effort as they were able, I really cannot (and probably should not) express the deeper feelings in their hearts or the struggles they might have faced. No doubt, they each have their own story to tell and I do not mean to preempt their doing so. I have, however, sought and received permission to tell our family story from each of them. They are willing, in the hope that our tale can be a blessing to someone.

Our adopted daughter Faith is at the center of this story and is its most vulnerable character. She appears first as an abandoned child and later I share some details from her bonding and attachment struggles. I had these details down on paper long ago but did not want to share them before Faith was old enough to give her serious consent and support. She and I have spoken about this at length and she has expressed her desire for the story to be told so other kids can be adopted and adopting families can be helped.

May our God get all the glory for this and may he use Faith's story for the good of the millions who still wait on their forever families.

## CHAPTER ONE: IN MADAGASCAR

I thought the devil himself must be involved. Who or what else could have so terrified the hearts of moms and dads that they could leave their babies out in the jungle to starve or be eaten by some wild animal? I felt ill. Those kids needed someone who would care for them. I wrote in my journal:

"Perhaps one day we will rescue one of these needy children and bring him into our own family."

This was the first I had seriously considered the possibility of adoption. It was January 1996 and the beginning of a 12-year journey.

* * * * *

"Look at that guy! He's naked," our new friend, Fin, exclaimed during our tour through the slum of downtown Antananarivo. Fin and his wife Catherine were Danish missionaries who had befriended us shortly after we arrived in the city to work with Africa Inland Mission. They were taking us on an after-dinner drive through the heart of our new hometown. The aforementioned naked man was lying on his stomach right in the middle of a crumbling sidewalk that was packed with people. It had been dark for about an hour and it seemed the masses of homeless were all searching for a spot to settle in along the side of the street.

It was evident there is no social safety net in Madagascar. Some of the men, women, and children starting little cooking fires at the side of the road may have been dwelling in their own apartment just a couple of months before. The man of the house might have lost his job and there was no work to be found. The family would begin selling off possessions to pay the bills and buy food. Luxuries like televisions and refrigerators would go first. Next the living room furniture, dining table, and then the beds. Finally, smaller possessions such as the family dishes and linens would be sold. When it all ran out, they would be on the street. It's not that friends and family were unwilling to help, just that they were rarely any better off. The streets were filled with families.

Fin pulled the station wagon over and called out to someone in the crowd. A little boy, maybe five years old, came over to the car window. He and Fin spoke in hushed Malagasy for a moment, Fin slipped the little boy a few coins, and we drove on.

"Who was that boy?" I asked.

"Just some kid that Catherine and I met here on the street," answered Fin. "We bought those clothes for him and every now and then we sneak him a little bit of money. We've got to be careful though. If someone saw us give him money, he might get beat up and robbed."

"Does he have any family that you know of?" I asked.

"Probably. There are lots of families living out here. Thousands I would say."

"You mean thousands of people?"

"No," Fin replied, "thousands of families."

I looked back through the crowd to see if I could get a glimpse of the little boy again. He was gone. We continued on in the car, heading off to find dessert in a hotel while countless mothers and fathers tried to get their children off to sleep where there were no beds. Even worse, some parentless children were tucking themselves into old boxes without any idea what their tomorrow would be like.

* * * * *

When we married in the summer of 1990, we had only the faintest idea of what would be next. Jennifer and I each had temporary cleaning jobs at the college I attended, and we had rented a small upstairs apartment a few miles from campus. The building that housed this apartment was not-so-affectionately called "the barn." Our cleaning jobs wrapped up right before school was to start, and we did not have prospects for anything new. As an old guy now, I look back on that situation with a certain amount of horror.

Nevertheless, our God was taking care of us. On registration day, completely out of the blue, I was offered a job working for the college plumber. I remember the interview well.

He asked, "Have you ever worked on a pump?"

"No, sir."

"Tell me about a time you repaired something."

"Uh…"

"Have you ever seen a screwdriver before?"

"Yes, sir!"

And with that, Larry the plumber decided to give me a chance. It was a real blessing. The job paid okay, came with good benefits, and included reduced tuition for Jennifer and me. The Lord treated us much better than we deserved, something he continues to do.

It was during the five years we were together in college that we began to sense a general call to serve the Lord. The words of Jesus to his first disciples sank deep into our hearts: "Come follow me, and I will make you fishers of men" (Mark 1:17). I did not know much, but I did know I wanted to be a follower of the Master Jesus. Jennifer did, too. However, we were not good at explaining exactly what we thought our calling from God was. This is still not a strong suit of mine. We knew, however, that we did like working and living among needy people.

After a couple of years in apartments on Lookout Mountain near the college, we bought a rundown house in a multi- racial, inner-city neighborhood in Chattanooga, Tennessee. As we fixed the old place up, we got to know a few of our neighbors. There was a blind woman who stood on the street waiting for the bus and a racist couple who built a 16-foot tall fence to prevent the older black man and his son next door from seeing into their yard. At the end of the block, a lonely old man lived in a small, extremely roach infested apartment. I would visit and help him clean up a little. I'd try to act natural while working in the kitchen, scrubbing the sink, and squashing bugs. This was where we began to define what God had in store for us. We felt called by God to help show his mercy to people that were difficult to be around.

With this fuzzy sense of purpose, after I graduated in May 1995, we sold our (much improved) little house in the city along with most of our belongings and headed out to Africa. We had read, "Foxes have holes, and birds of the air have nests, but the Son of Man has nowhere to lay his head" (Mt. 8:20). I know it is not really for everyone, but it seemed to us that selling what we had and trekking to the developing world was an easy way for us to try being like Jesus. At that time, Madagascar was one of the world's poorest and most unstable nations. It continues to be so.

\* \* \* \* \*

It was almost Christmas in Africa. Jennifer and I had developed a routine of language and culture learning that was occupying us almost full time. Life in another country was quite an adventure, not only for us, but also for our two little boys, Joshua and Andrew. Joshua was three years old and Andrew was one. They did not know they were in Madagascar. Even if they had, I do not think it would have made much of an impression on them. Like most children that age, they were happy so long as mom and dad were happy.

Still though, I worried sometimes about the bedroom full of toys they had left behind. To compensate for this, I brought a stack of cardboard boxes into our apartment and we made toys together. We made buildings and all kinds of vehicles. My favorite was an Aircraft Carrier complete with fighter jets and a helicopter. Still though, playing with cardboard was a far cry from a

Little Tikes toy box full of noisy, battery-operated, American toys. I decided I was going to make up for this on Christmas day!

Not too far from our house was one of the two supermarkets in our city of over one million residents. The French developers of this market had installed a traffic light at the entrance to their parking lot. It was the only traffic light I had seen in the city. Fin told me they had tried to use the light to manage traffic, but no one would pay attention to it. The rule of the road in Madagascar was that bigger vehicles went first and everyone went fast. As Jennifer and I drove up in front of the Giant Score Supermarket to do some Christmas shopping, the traffic light simply flashed, defeated, in yellow.

Inside the store was a stark contrast to the tattered city outside. The shiny tile floors, colorful shelves lined with imported products, and the continuously playing Madonna album made it feel like we had landed on another planet. Jennifer and I made it back to an aisle lined with plastic toys. They did not seem like the best quality to me, but they would have to do. Into the cart went Batman on a motorcycle, a fire truck, construction vehicles, balls, games, and even a couple of big plastic tubs that would become miniature swimming pools. The total for all this loot came to just over $100. That was a lot for us, but I was certain it would be worth it when we saw our kids' faces on Christmas morning. Feeling like super-dad, I pushed our cartload of Chinese-made plastic and batteries out towards the car.

Of course, when you are tall and white in the middle of a country full of shorter dark-skinned folks who seem to have nothing but time, you never go unnoticed. (My wife and I are not really tall, but we appeared so in Madagascar). As soon as we started for the car, a handful of men came over to help us. They really did intend to be helpful and they were perfect gentlemen. They took the cart from me so I would not need to push and they took the bags that Jennifer carried. When we arrived at the little white Toyota wagon, they loaded everything into the car and held the doors as we climbed in. We felt like royalty! All for just a few cents tip.

As I slipped my key into the ignition, I watched our band of helpers retreating back across the parking lot. Their clothes hung on them like rags. "Why even bother wearing that shirt?" I thought. "There's hardly any material left. You see more skin than cloth!" Starting the car and getting ready to back out, I still stared at the men. Thinking about the shopping cart they had just unloaded, I did some quick math in my head. I said to Jennifer, "Those guys would have to work four months to buy those junky toys we just got. And that's if they had a job."

As I pulled the car up at the ever-flashing yellow light, I looked over at the chain-link fence separating the supermarket lot from the adjacent field. A half-dozen children stood watching our car. Only a couple had shirts. None had shoes. Their bellies were swollen with hunger. But my boys would play with Batman on Christmas day.

* * * * *

Sometimes we went to a local Malagasy church, but it was difficult for us because of the language barriers. That is, of course, not to mention our inability to hold our one and three-year-old boys while balancing our rear-ends on a four-inch wide bench for a couple of hours. Thankfully, there was a small English-speaking church that met in an old building downtown. Most Sunday mornings would find Jennifer, Joshua, Andrew, and me climbing into an old taxi and heading to this fellowship.

The taxi itself was an experience. The drivers rented the taxis by the day, for a set fee. Any money they made over that amount was profit. Like all good businessmen, the Malagasy taxi drivers were always watching their bottom line. They were particularly conscious of fuel efficiency. Whenever we came to one of the many hills in Antananarivo, they would shut the engine off and coast down. Since they had to purchase their own gasoline, they developed an ingenious method to make sure they did not leave any of it in the tank when they returned their vehicles at the end of the day. Most drivers carried along a little plastic jug of gas to set on the front floorboard of the car with a fuel line stuck inside. In this way, they bypassed the gas tank altogether. I was always troubled by the way these little flammable containers sat in such close proximity to the car's ashtray. Every driver smoked cigarettes like a chimney. Thankfully, we were always safe in traffic, even if we did arrive at our destination smelling like we had just splashed on some petroleum cologne after spending the evening in a pool hall.

One hot January morning, Jennifer and I arrived at the little English church, dropped the kids in a make-shift Sunday School, and sat down to enjoy some fellowship with other attendees before the service began. The "sanctuary" where we sat was a large empty room with peeling paint on the block walls. In the center of the room there were about 20 folding chairs formed in a circle. Jennifer and I grabbed seats next to a middle-aged couple with a newborn baby.

We already knew most of the people there and said hello as they entered. Two of the families were part of our mission board, the Africa Inland Mission. One family was from England and the other from South Africa. There was also another couple from South Africa who were with Child Evangelistic

Fellowship. The couple we sat by were Americans serving with Bible Study Fellowship.

This BSF couple had our special attention that particular morning because of the cute little Malagasy baby in the woman's arms. The child's brown skin was a giveaway that she was not born into the very Caucasian family.

"That is a cute baby you have there," Jennifer said.

"She certainly is cute! She's a rescued forest baby," answered the woman.

"A forest baby?"

"Oh, don't you know?" The woman shifted the baby on her knee. "Some of the locals outside the city - not all of course, but some - are still very superstitious. If a baby is born into a family on the wrong day, for example, or if there are twins, it is considered a very bad omen. In that case, the father will take the child out into the bush and abandon him there. One of our friends is part of a team who walks through the forest looking for babies that otherwise would have been left out to die. That's where this little girl came from. We're going to be her foster parents for a while."

"You mean, they really just leave the babies out in the woods?" I asked.

"They sure do. It's a real problem. Some of the Malagasy people are still enslaved to the old tribal religions of their ancestors."

"What will happen with this little one now?" Jennifer wanted to know.

"Well, we're not sure yet. Adoption is very difficult, but we hope someone can take her. If not, then we'll just hold onto her as long as we can."

Someone had just begun some music on a guitar. The service was starting. Jennifer and I considered the little brown face with a feeling of thanksgiving mixed with grief for the baby's situation and those forest babies that might not be found.

\* \* \* \* \*

Later that month I sat at the plain wooden desk, the centerpiece of the workroom in our apartment. It was cluttered with papers, a desktop copier, and computer. A huge open window filled one wall. Outside there was a tropical tree of some variety, which was chocked full of chameleons. These 12-inch lizards were so well camouflaged that you had to stare at the tree for quite a while before you started to see them. But I was focused on writing in a small paper book. I really wanted to keep a journal of all the experiences we were having on this exotic island.

On that January day, I was writing about the forest babies. After summarizing the plight of these children, I began to think about how they were rejected by their own families. It was then that I postulated about the devil's work in it all and seriously considered becoming an adoptive parent for the first time.

## CHAPTER TWO: IN AMERICA

"Okay, crank it up!"

Joshua was happy to spin the handle of the post holding the trailer tongue off the ground. His brother Andrew and I watched as the weight of our 26-foot travel trailer came down on the hitch. When the crank could go no further, the three of us stepped back onto the lawn and admired our rig. Although the tow vehicle was already six years old, its classic Chevy Suburban lines were highlighted by glossy black paint and beefy-looking off-road tires. To the boys and I, the truck looked great with the nearly new Jayco Camper. They were part of our little piece of the American dream. Any guilt I felt about the cost of these toys was mitigated by the fact that, nice as they were, they were always among the smallest and most modest in the campgrounds.

Camping had become a great way to take our growing family on vacation. We could no longer fit in a motel room. Joshua was now 13 and his brother Andrew 11. The Lord had blessed us with four other children too: Jacob, Simon Peter, Elijah, and the youngest, Grace. With five boys and one little girl, we had become quite a crowd!

Of course, we were not hitching up a camper in Antananarivo, Madagascar. Sadly, we stayed there for less than a year. There had been some major disagreements on our ministry team. Furthermore, the job I had gone to do was not really needed or wanted by the team leaders. No doubt, my own immaturity further strained our relationship with coworkers. So, despite our love for life on the mission field, we found ourselves back in the States late in 1996 with little idea where to turn.

After several months of working odd jobs, Jennifer and I decided to move to St. Louis, so I could study at Covenant Theological Seminary. Seminary was a great experience for our family. We made lots of friends and grew in our understanding of God and His Word. After our time there, I began teaching Bible and History at a Christian high school in Huntsville, Alabama. In addition to teaching the kids during the week, I had many opportunities to preach at local churches on the weekends. Eventually, the Lord confirmed in our hearts a call to serve in a local church ministry. I left teaching and became the full-time pastor of North Hills Church in November 2003.

By 2006, we were actively enjoying a growing church ministry, we had beautiful kids, a four-bedroom brick house in the suburbs (complete with in-ground pool), two cars, a camper, and a typical American golden retriever. We really were enjoying the Evangelical, Christian, American dream. However, Jennifer and I never felt comfortable with where we were in life. It was as if we did not completely fit in. We often referred to it as a "missions bug" which we had picked up in Madagascar and never lost.

This "bug" came out strongly each year at our church's World Missions Conference. The conference was our favorite event on the church calendar. Each year we had a keynote speaker, special music, and a variety of local and international missionaries who were supported by the church. In our first year at North Hills, we began a faith promise giving program. With faith promise, individuals or families are encouraged to make a promise to give to God beyond what they think they can give. The promise is made only to God and the giver trusts that He will provide the money to pass on to the mission fund. It was fantastic to see how the Lord provided. Using this method, our church missions giving increased by 300% in just two years. God was teaching us that He could provide.

In February 2006, we were enjoying another of these missions conferences. Listening to our special speaker, Dr. Frank Barker, and hearing the reports from missionaries was a great blessing to us, as always. It was so exciting to hear how God was moving among the homeless people living in the streets of our own town, of how the gospel was being broadcast into communist nations in Southeast Asia, and how Ukrainian orphans were receiving medical attention from Christian nurses. As much as I loved serving as a pastor, I could sense the urgency and importance of what these missionaries were doing. Each night when we got home, Jennifer and I would talk about how we felt the pull towards missions. We wanted to do something for the nations!

There was even more going on in Jennifer's mind though. The weekend of that conference she wrote in her journal, "I don't know if God worked in others the same way, but Stephen and I ended the weekend with great excitement about missions, both local and abroad. What Stephen doesn't realize is that whenever I get really excited about missions, the Lord puts adoption foremost in my mind and heavily upon my heart. This time was no exception!"

Apparently, Jennifer had a kind of "double-bug." She was not only interested in reaching out to the needy souls of faraway places. She wanted to bring some of those needy souls right into our family. This was not a new thought for her either. She had dreamed of adopting even while she was a child and thought seriously about it early in our marriage.

However, it was during our church missions conference at the end of February 2006 that Jennifer was certain God was calling us to adopt a child. "Now I need God to tell my husband as soon as possible," she wrote in her journal.

Jennifer was determined to be God's instrument in letting me know! She told me she was thinking we should adopt a child from another country, bought a big book that told the story of one family's adoption, and began reading it aloud to our kids in the living room. My response was one of loving, husbandly, pastoral caution.

We had just finished closing on the new house, camper, and four-wheel drive dream vehicle. While we lived in a nice neighborhood and managed to blend in well among the space and missile industry engineers who made up most of our town's population, I was a pastor with little or no savings. We basically lived paycheck to paycheck. Furthermore, we did already have six children to feed, clothe, educate, and provide with health care. To me, we just did not fit the profile for people who would jet off to China and bring back a needy child. That kind of thing was for the Daddy Warbucks of the world.

"I'll pray for you," Jennifer said. And she did just that. She also talked me into reading a book, the same the rest of the family had been reading together. *The Waiting Child* was about a little girl named Jaclyn who was adopted from China by the author, Cindy Champnella (Champnella 2004). This little one, while only four years old, was deeply concerned about a younger boy who she took care of while living at an orphanage in her birth country. Although she was little more than a baby herself, Jaclyn refused to give up on the idea that her new mom and dad needed to go back to China and get him, too! Against all odds, contrary to what the family felt they had resources to accomplish, and despite the experts saying they could never get the Chinese government to cooperate, the family succeeded in bringing Jaclyn's little friend to America. The two children did not end up in the same home, but they became cousins when Mrs. Champnella's sister adopted the baby boy. Closing this book after a quick read, I found it a little harder to make excuses and joined Jennifer in prayer.

On the last day of February, as we prepared for bed, the two of us prayed together for the first time specifically about the possibility of adopting a child. Meanwhile, somewhere far away in Asia, there was a little baby just starting out in life. At that time, she was fed, held, and loved like so many children. Of course, she had no idea she would soon become one of the millions of orphans in the world. And no one but God himself could have ever guessed her adoptive mom and dad were praying for her.

## CHAPTER THREE:
## LEARNING ABOUT ADOPTION

"What do your kids think?"

"I've heard it's really hard."

"Don't you worry about whether you'll love the child like your own?"

"Did you see that news story about the birth parents who came and took their child back from the family who had adopted him?"

"I hear it's very expensive."

Silence.

These were the reactions we got from many folks when we announced our intention to adopt. I cannot really judge them for these cold responses; it took me a while to come to grips with the idea myself. The thing is, the Bible commands us to "look after orphans" (James 1:27) and Christians are adopted by God himself (Eph. 1:4-6). That being the case, it is strange how difficult it is for us to embrace adoption. I think perhaps there is some great spiritual evil that is opposed to the rescue of children. I know that sounds like overstatement at this point, but perhaps the pages to follow will change your mind.

Not everyone was dour about our announcement. Our dear friends at church, Aaron and Erica Hammond, were interested in the needs of orphans and would eventually adopt a child from China. They sensed the Lord was calling them to use their gifts and resources for His glory by promoting adoption as a means of helping needy children. Aaron and Erica were a constant source of encouragement to us.

We are also blessed to have Christian parents who understand our desire to do what is pleasing to the Lord even though other people may think we are nuts. My parents, Bob and Susan, and Jennifer's parents, Doug and Jamie, committed to pray for us as we sought the Lord's leading. My brother Matthew, his wife Christa and their two daughters were also prayer warriors on our behalf. I share this not only because I am thankful and proud of our family, but because of my firm belief that their prayers were essential in helping us through the days ahead. God used our adoption journey to teach me the significance and power of prayer in ways I had never experienced before.

* * * * *

We had to have a home study. Yikes! This meant that a state approved social worker would study our family and determine whether we were "okay" or not. Can you imagine? Despite the pictures of happy kids and pets that cluttered our living room, I was not certain if we could pass muster. Don't get me wrong, my wife and kids are awesome. It's just that I was afraid we might not be typical enough for state approval.

For example, our kids had a bedroom in the garage; we did, however, eventually replace the garage door with a brick wall and picture window. At first, the room was very, um… garage-like. Half of it was made up like a bedroom for Joshua and Andrew. The other half was a pile of boxes and other stored items. Joshua still likes to talk about how I would wake them up in the morning by hitting the garage door opener, thus removing one exterior wall of their bedroom.

As I mentioned already, we were also not the most financially sound family. The Lord has rescued us repeatedly from debt and low salaries as a Christian school teacher and pastor. In fact, we always had much nicer things than seemed possible. Somehow though, this made our lack of savings and resources seem even more pathetic. Factoring in the mortgage, vehicles, and camper gave us a net worth of about zero.

Furthermore, we had some strong, conservative opinions about how to raise kids. I am not ashamed of this in the least, but I was wondering what the social worker would think. Yes, we made our children go to church every time the doors were open. Yes, they only went to Christian schools or were homeschooled. Yes, all the kids did chores at the house and in the yard (I worked them like farmhands). Yes, we spanked their behinds when they did not do what we told them to do. No, they did not watch whatever they liked on TV. And we had absolutely no intention of changing any of those things.

With all this in mind, I must admit I thought our adoption plan would never make it past the home study stage. Driving two hours to the office of Lifeline Children's Services in Birmingham, Alabama felt like a waste of time. "They are not going to like us," I thought.

We were soon sitting in a reception room across from a social worker. She was a Christian and a very unassuming, kind woman who quickly put us at ease. Somehow or another she even brought up spanking and assured us there was no law against it in the State of Alabama. She gave us a brief overview of the process. We would fill out approximately 28,000 forms. Maybe she did not say that exact number, but she may as well have. These would give her information about our past, about our family style, about our finances, about plans for a potential adopted child, and so on. We would also provide references and read several books about adoption issues. We would meet with her a few times and there would be a home visit to inspect our property. I was glad I had recently replaced the garage door with a wall.

We also learned at this meeting about the complex maze of government paperwork that would be necessary. Not just our government, but also the government of the country we would adopt from. In our case that would be China, or so it seemed. They would review our police records (and to think I had assumed I did not have one), the government would fingerprint us, and we would have to provide all our personal information to Uncle Sam and the Chinese bureaucracy. I was hoping Jennifer understood this part, because my eyes were soon glazed over while the social worker spoke of LOI's, CIS, CCAA, ABI's, USCIS, I-797's, I-600's and a stream of other letters and numbers.

One number snapped me back to reality though - $17,000. I had to interrupt the stream of consonant/vowel combinations that were flowing in the conversation. "How much was that again?"

"Well, the estimated total cost should come to around $17,000," she said matter of fact like, "but don't worry, it is not all due at once."

I was hoping I had just enough money for lunch and gas back to Huntsville, but I said something like, "Oh, okay, no problem."

When the meeting had ended and we were pulling away in our car, I said to Jennifer, "Did she really say $17,000? Wow, that's a lot!"

"Yes, but if God wants us to adopt, then he will provide," Jennifer responded. Her words were convicting to me. I knew she was right.

"Okay. We will pray and you can take care of the paperwork. I'll worry about the money."

\* \* \* \* \*

As time went on, I began to get a better perspective on the cost of an international adoption. I realized that the entire adoption could cost our family less than our Suburban and Camper did. That really put things into perspective. You may not see it as clearly as I did, but camping had become a big hobby for us. It was an expensive investment, but we really loved it! I honestly think our trips out were good for us. Nevertheless, once I had learned about the cost of adoption, I could not look at our truck and camper without thinking that an orphaned child, an eternal soul no less, could be placed in a loving family for the same cost. How do you compare the two?

I noticed when I shared our adoption plans with friends at church, the conversation would eventually settle on the cost. When I told them it might cost from $17,000 to $25,000, they often looked shocked! In fact, some would even speak up, "So much money! Where will you get it?" Later we would all head out to the parking lot and climb into our cars. Most of them had new price tags of between $15,000 and $40,000. Where do we get all that money?

# CHAPTER 4:
# HEARTSTRINGS AND HEARTBREAK

I always enjoyed pulling up in front of a store or restaurant in our family vehicle. Anyone who bothered to notice would see Jennifer and I climb out with a couple of kids. Then they would see two more kids wiggle out of the back seat, and then another, and still one more! It is so much fun having a big family. You are never lonely in our house. No one sits around talking about how bored they are. There is always someone nearby. This is great when you want to organize a game of football or when you need to move a piece of furniture. It is also exciting to remember that each child is an eternal soul created in the image of God and therefore able to make a big difference for His glory in the world. Unfortunately, not everyone sees it this way. I wish I had a nickel for every time someone looked at our family and said, "Don't you know what causes that?" Oh well, I'll stick with God's opinion that children are a blessing.

Do not get me wrong. I think the number of children a couple has is a very personal decision. No one should prescribe how many children a couple should have or not have. It's just that I am saddened by the reasons some people give for not having more kids. Sometimes, it sounds to me like men and women just do not want to give up the time it takes to invest in children or they do not believe the God who gives them children is able to take care of them.

When we first began talking with the adoption agency, we learned that our family size was going to be a challenge. Most countries limited the number of children they thought were acceptable in a home. We quickly discovered, however, that one Eastern European country and one South American country had no family size limits for adoption. Also, both countries were full of overcrowded orphanages and exploited children. This was exactly the kind of need that we wanted to address.

There were a couple of difficulties though. At that time, to adopt from Eastern Europe, potential parents had to travel there and stay for over a month. Then, they would need to leave for a while and return later to pick up their child. This would not only prove difficult for us because of work and family responsibilities, it sounded torturous to meet your new child, get to know and love her, and then go away without final confirmation of the adoption.

If we went to South America, the process was faster (although it still required two separate trips), but the base cost of adoption there was over $35,000. Furthermore, the government in that country had a reputation for corruption.

This was the first I had thought about corruption in international adoption. I could not help thinking the first country wanted foreigners to stay so long because they would spend more money on hotels, restaurants, and a mysterious list of government fees. Likewise, the enormous cost of adoption in our second choice seemed dodgy. The government there pocketed nearly half the adoption cost. I wondered how much of that went toward the care of children. As I saw it, many of the decision makers in these countries (and we have since learned in many more) exploited the plight of needy children to line their pockets.

There are different ways to respond to this. One approach is to say, because the systems are corrupt, we should avoid trying. It does seem necessary at times to avoid adopting from certain countries or specific locations within a country. Nevertheless, I think a better approach is to work within the legal system as best as you possibly can. Read and learn about how it is supposed to work, use a trusted agency or lawyer, be diligent and involved. The children are worth the extra effort. Even though government officials and orphanage workers may be guilty of abuse, we must remember there are millions of real, parentless, children in the world. Someone needs to reach out to them, stick up for them, and do all that is possible to bring them into good families. Every child deserves a loving home!

It is also worth mentioning that bad news is always the most popular. The good news of successful adoptions is not told nearly enough. Just because there are bad and sad stories out there, does not mean that legal, honorable, wonderful adoptions are not taking place. They happen every day, all over the world. No doubt there are government officials and orphanage workers worldwide who toil constantly for the good of the needy children in their care. Even as we oppose corruption and abuse, those people who are working hard for the sake of orphans ought to be recognized and honored.

We were spared the difficulty of deciding about Eastern Europe or South America when our adoption agency called and told us we had qualified for a "family size waiver" to adopt from China. To get the waiver we needed to be willing to adopt a special needs child. This meant the child could have a wide range of medical issues, from minor things to serious conditions. We willingly, but prayerfully, accepted this offer on March 17, 2006 and spent the next month completing paperwork for the US and

Chinese governments. Finally, on Monday, April 24 we received a very exciting email. In it were the name, health records, and even photographs of the little girl who was to be our daughter.

Ji Ruxian had been born sometime in June 2005. She lived in an orphanage in Chengdu, China. There was no information about her biological parents. Ji Ruxian had a minor heart condition and it was supposed she would need some special medical care. Otherwise, she was healthy. Along with her medical records, there was a picture of a serious faced girl sitting on the floor in a pink bundle of clothes.

Jennifer wrote on our blog, "When we shared her photo with friends and family, several people commented that she looked like a St. John baby with almond shaped eyes. It is amazing how you can fall totally in love with a child just through a photo." This was so true. Seeing the picture of this little one brought the whole process to life for me. Suddenly it was no longer an ideological campaign to meet the needs of a child or make a difference in the world. There was something very personal about seeing that photo. Here was a real girl, without parents, living in a cold block building in central China and she was going to come and stay with us!

The picture gave us a burst of energy! We shared it with everyone. Our friend from church, Erica, put it on little postcards and prepared a fundraiser.

Jennifer and I pursued our home study in earnest. We filled out every form as quickly as we could and stayed up late each night trying to get everything together at record-breaking speed. We did tons of required reading, went to the police station for fingerprinting, continued to meet with our social worker for interviews, and by May 22, we reached a stopping place where we were just waiting to hear from China. We knew adoptions could take a long time, but we were determined it would not be because of us! We could not wait for the day that Faith Ruxian St. John would be settled in her Alabama home. Of course, we do not always know what twists and turns lay in the road ahead.

* * * * *

I was sitting in my office at North Hills Church when the phone rang. Between sobs, Jennifer managed to get out, "Please come home, they said no!"

"No? No to what?" I asked.

"We can't adopt Ji Ruxian."

"I'll be right home. I love you."

This was a strange feeling. As a pastor, I had received calls from people who have lost loved ones to accidents and even suicide. The feeling I had rushing out to the car and heading home was just like that. Somebody was suddenly gone. I had to keep reminding myself that Ji Ruxian was not dead. In fact, for all I knew, she had been selected for adoption by someone else. Still, the sudden void in our hearts was very real.

When I arrived at home, the whole house was in mourning. A young lady from church had been spending the day with Jennifer, but she sat now in the living room with our children. All the kids were sad. I should mention here, they prayed each day for the adoption and were in it with their mom and dad 100 percent. They studied the picture of the girl who was to be their sister over and over again. They trusted that our family was doing something that pleased God. This sudden event was very confusing to them.

I sent our friend from church home and found Jennifer in our bedroom. She was crushed, I could tell. We went through the kind of routine that many of you know. Holding each other, crying, and just telling each other it would be okay. In my mind I was ready to submit to the fact that we tried, but God did not want us to adopt. We had thrown ourselves into the process, but He had said no. After a few hours, though, Jennifer spoke clearly and bravely. She said something like, "I guess Ji Ruxian wasn't the one. We need to pray for her to be placed in a good family. And we will keep praying for our little girl who is out there somewhere."

Although women are sometimes referred to as the weaker sex, my wife can be powerful. That evening as we lay in bed after praying about Ji Ruxian, our kids, and our grief, I thought about the amazing work of God in Jennifer's heart. If you have seen someone who is clearly "called by God" to do something, then you understand the strength of resolve in my wife. The crushing news of the morning had turned into trust in God and determination to press on by evening.

## CHAPTER FIVE: MOVING AHEAD

As we moved into the summer of 2006, we continued to pray for a new opportunity to adopt from China. However, on August 9, we learned that China would not allow our family to adopt at all. Apparently, there was some debate behind the scenes between our adoption agency and the Chinese government about whether we had ever been approved for a "family size waiver." We will never know why things did not work out with China or why we lost the referral for little Ji Ruxian. We do know, though, that God was working all things together for good. After only a few days, Jennifer firmly announced that we would find our little girl in Vietnam.

"Not so fast!" I thought. Only a few weeks before, we were telling everyone that our little girl was in China. I just knew people would start to think we were even nuttier than they already did. How could Jennifer say she knows where our little girl is now? As a pastor, I did a bit of counseling. Often, I had told others, "If it's not clearly stated in the word of

God, then it's dangerous to say you know God wants you to do a specific thing."

"I'll pray for you," Jennifer said. Hmm…

About three days later, as I was drifting off to sleep on Friday night, Jennifer lay awake praying that God would confirm in our hearts if we should adopt from Vietnam. I awoke early on Saturday August 19, unable to sleep in, which was unusual for a Saturday morning. After starting the coffee pot, I headed into the living room and sat down to pray. I knew I needed to pray about the adoption, but as soon as the words "Our Father" came, I was unable to continue. A picture flashed through my mind from years before. I could not make it go away. All I could do was cry.

Now this was not a theophany or some kind of extra-biblical revelation. It was a real picture I remembered in my head. I loved books growing up (and still do). I have fond memories of sitting in the downstairs of my childhood home and looking at all kinds of books. On the table in the den, there was a collection of coffee table books, full of fascinating pictures from history. Sailing ships, presidents, castles, and soldiers filled the pages. But somewhere in all that was the one picture I remembered as I prayed on that Saturday morning. Many of you will know the picture I am talking about.

It is haunting and yet hard to stop looking at. The picture is of a group of children running up a road. Behind them are soldiers and a vast fire burning. All the children are crying out in pain and fear. There are no parents around, only soldiers armed with rifles. One little girl has no clothing on; an explosion burned them off. The children are, of course, in Vietnam ("The KIM Foundation International: Healing Children of War" 2018).

As Jennifer was still sleeping, and I was trying to pray, the image of that naked, hurting, frightened little girl filled my mind. I remembered then my thoughts from years ago as a boy in my den. "Why doesn't somebody help her?" In that moment, I knew Jennifer's prayer for me had been answered. Vietnam it would be. There was a little girl there who needed our help, who needed a home.

\* \* \* \* \*

The agency we were using in Alabama did not handle adoptions from Vietnam. Undeterred, Jennifer began to search the Internet for all possible information on adopting from there. She found blogs, good news, bad news, agencies, recommendations, warnings, etc. Eventually she settled on the name of a lawyer in Indiana who was helping a few families adopt from Vietnam. "Let's use her!" Jennifer announced.

"But we don't even know her. She's just some lady on the Internet! You can't just call people like that up out of the blue. Plus, she's in Indiana and we are getting a home study from the State of Alabama. Not to mention the fact she's a lawyer!"

A few moments later, we were ringing the phone of Michele Jackson, attorney, in Indianapolis. She talked fast, but we could sense she was passionate about helping needy kids find good homes and she agreed to help us. It was no fault of hers, but we also learned that changing from China to Vietnam would cost us quite a bit more money. Oh well, somehow, it did not seem so important anymore. What kind of price tag would you place on your son or daughter?

Before August ended, we were deep into paperwork for adopting from Vietnam. We also continued our Alabama home study with the same agency we had been using. Apparently, it would still work for our approval to adopt, even though we would not be using that agency to find a child. We were cleared by the Alabama Bureau of Investigation, the Department of Human Resources, and fingerprinted by Citizenship and Immigration Services. Lots of money passed through our hands, but the Lord was providing, one step at a time.

* * * * *

Another amazing thing happened that summer. Jennifer loved to read about adoption on the Internet. There are thousands of stories about ordinary Christian families doing the extraordinary by adopting children. Many of these are recorded on blogs that make for entertaining and encouraging reading. One day, Jennifer ran across a blog about a family who was adopting a little girl from China. Immediately, Jennifer recognized the photograph of the girl they were hoping to bring home. It was Ji Ruxian! A half hour of reading reassured us that this new family, the Pierces, loved Jesus deeply and they would make a wonderful home for the little girl who might have been ours.

We resisted the temptation to contact them and tell them we had almost adopted the little girl. We were certain that would seem really weird. However, after weeks of following their blog and beginning to feel that we knew them better, Jennifer sent Tina Pierce an email introducing herself. The results were amazing. Our two families quickly became friends and prayer partners as we pursued our adoptions.

Later in the summer, shortly after Ji Ruxian arrived in America with her new family, we were invited to her second birthday party! As I stood on the patio and watched this dear child opening a huge pile of presents, I wondered about the way our God works. While it was not His plan for her to be part of our family, He did allow us the privilege of praying for her earnestly. Only the Lord knows what kind of spiritual battles were fought around Ji Ruxian as He placed her in a loving Christian home. May He get all the glory and may she be one of millions who are brought into families where the gospel is taught and the love of Christ is on display each day!

## CHAPTER SIX: A SURPRISE CALL

The year 2007 opened with us preparing for another missions conference at North Hills Church. Once again, Jennifer and I were filled with energy as we thought about God's call to share the love and message of Jesus with all the nations. Of course, this year our thoughts and prayers were directed particularly toward Asia, with special attention given to China and Vietnam. In the weeks leading up to the conference, I think Jennifer and I knew in our hearts that change was on the horizon.

The call to leave our comfort zone was growing more intense. Missionary biographies were scattered all over our living room end-tables and bedroom nightstands. It wasn't just mom and dad either. The kids loved the stories about Gladys Aylward, Adoniram Judson, Bruce Olson, Don Richardson, and Brother Andrew. Meanwhile we were learning more about the needs in Asia as we prayed for our friends who were adopting from China and for our planned adoption from Vietnam.

We had met a wonderful family who used our lawyer, Michele, to help them adopt from Vietnam. The Frank family had developed a DVD of the whole experience. In one section, the adoptive father, Pete, goes from place to place as they tour the country and asks various men, women, and children if they had ever heard of Jesus Christ. They all said no! We watched this video over and over again. My kids asked to see it often because we had so few good pictures of the cities and people of Vietnam. This meant I got to see Pete Frank's "man on the street" interviews over and over again. I began to think about an intersection of two callings. One new, a call to adopt, and one call which had been lying dormant from long ago when we sensed the Lord leading us to Madagascar. It was a call to the mission field.

This was not a convenient time. We were deep into the adoption process, busy raising six children, and leading a young and growing church congregation. When our favorite Bible teacher from college, Dr. Henry Krabbendam, agreed to be the main speaker at our missions conference, I decided to share what was on our hearts with him. We loved Dr. K (as we called him) and felt he was used by God to plant a seed of interest for missions in our heart years ago. He spent every summer ministering in Uganda and since his retirement from teaching full-time, he had bought property there to develop a Christian training school.

Dr. K and I took a short break from the conference schedule and headed out for sandwiches at the local Subway. Dr. K greeted all the people in the restaurant with his loud Dutch accented English and invited each of them to our church, which was humbling because I had never done so. Once this scene was over, I got us some subs, and Dr. K crammed his almost seven-foot-tall frame into a little booth. Once seated and quiet, I told him that Jennifer and I were thinking of making a move to serve out of the country. His first reply was anticlimactic.

"Well, one thing is for sure," he said, "you will find out if you should do that or not. This is a good sandwich."

"Is that it?" I wondered to myself. I was ready to listen to some profound statement about how great it was that we wanted to reach out with the gospel. Unsatisfied, I began to spew forth a string of comments about the needy people in other countries and how we wanted to share the love of Christ with them. Finally, Dr. K's eyes flashed and he said, "The problem with American Christians coming to our country (I assumed he meant Uganda) is they mess up everything. In Uganda the Christians are different. I walk down the street and people will cry out from their shops, 'Hello and praise the Lord!' I'll answer, 'Praise the Lord!' If I preach in church for just one hour, people complain and ask for more. Has that ever happened to you here? Ugandans have suffered a lot, but when they become born again, they are happy and zealous for the gospel. They share it without reservation and they have a holy lifestyle to match. The Americans who come to us are tight lipped about their faith and mired in their own sordid pop culture. We do not need people like that."

After this outburst, Dr. K went promptly back to chewing his sandwich. I stared pensively out the window. Although he did not say he was speaking to me directly, I could not help but think he had me in mind. After all, he was the one who had invited the Subway staff to the church where I was pastor, not me. We never really talked about this subject again, but one of his messages at the conference offered some hope. He said, "If you think God is calling you to do something, commit to do it, unless God stops you!"

\* \* \* \* \*

In April, I was invited to preach for the Men's Conference at Scofield Memorial Church in Dallas, Texas. There were seminary professors and other eminently qualified speakers at this event. I was there only because my brother was the pastor at Scofield. I did enjoy preaching and visiting my brother Matthew, his wife Christa, and their two wonderful daughters Emily and Katy. But a significant thing happened to me on the flight there and back.

A year or so before, at a pastors' meeting, I had been given a copy of John Piper's book *Don't Waste Your Life* (Piper 2003). It had sat on my shelf collecting dust for many months, but for some reason I decided to pick it up and read it on my trip to Dallas. It was hardly necessary to read much beyond the cover of the book. Piper writes, "You get one pass at life. That's all. Only one. And the lasting measure of that life is Jesus Christ (13)." He then challenges us to take risks for God, stop storing up so much treasure on the earth, and instead invest in heaven.

I read a lot of books, and as much as I like Dr. Piper, I am not sure what was so special about this one. However, I know the Lord really used it to help me refocus. I began to think about how I had spent so much time and energy on stuff over the past 10 years. Yes, I was a serious Christian, but the zeal for the lost and the needy that I felt so strongly years ago in Africa had faded away in the glare of shiny suburban American toys. Our whole culture is constantly telling us to make ourselves as comfortable and secure as possible. This, we are told, is the path to happiness. But I am not so sure it is true. What difference will it make at the end of our life if we had lots of money, a big house, a pool, a monster truck, and a camper? Piper quotes an old line, "Just one life, 'twill soon be past; only what's done for Christ will last."

I was so taken with these ideas that we began a *Don't Waste Your Life* Bible study in our house. Some of our good friends from church attended. I hope it was useful for them in their lives, but I know it made a big impact on us. The Lord had prepared Jennifer and I to take a risk for him. Crazy as it seemed, we decided we would become missionaries, unless God stopped us.

But we could not be regular missionaries. They must travel to different churches all the time and raise money. As a pastor, that would not work for me. I could not quit my job. Not only did we have a big family to feed, I needed to maintain a stable employment situation for our adoption home study to go through.

One Saturday evening in May, Jennifer and I started thinking about International Churches. I cannot remember why, but we started to think that perhaps I could be a pastor in another country at an international church, which could simply hire me to serve just like North Hills had. This was a novel idea, but we got down on our knees before bed that night and asked God, "Lord if there is an international church you would like for us to serve at, then please let us know."

The next day, after our Sunday evening worship service, a retired pastor and friend of ours approached me in the lobby of our church building. "Stephen," he said, "I want to tell you about this International Church in Jakarta, Indonesia that is looking for a pastor." I could have passed out right there. Nobody knew about the prayer Jennifer and I made the night before. We had never even discussed the idea with anyone. In fact, the previous evening was the first we had even talked about it between the two of us. The only other person who knew was God! Of course, I felt we had to at least consider the possibility.

\* \* \* \* \*

Three months later, I was on a plane headed to Jakarta, Indonesia. It was a good thing I was not the one flying the plane. Not only am I not a pilot, I only had a foggy idea of where Indonesia was. When we first heard about Jakarta, we had to go home and look for it on a map, even though more people live in the city of Jakarta than the entire state of Alabama.

Jennifer and I had contacted the Jakarta International Baptist Church the same week we heard about it from our friend and things heated up fast. The church wanted someone who loved to teach the Bible and we really wanted to serve God in an international context. A hundred emails went back and forth, interviews took place over the

Internet, and now here I was flying over so the church members and I could get a look at each other before the final decision was made.

The city of Jakarta, Indonesia defies description. It is truly an amazing place. It is the world's largest predominantly Muslim city, but it is also full of Western businesses and shops. It is a polluted and dirty city, but it also possesses natural beauty in trees and plants along with some of the cleanest and most sparkling malls and hotels I have ever seen. There is heart-rending poverty in Jakarta, right alongside mind-blowing wealth. You just have to experience it to understand. I fell in love with the city right away.

The church was also wonderful. Of course, it had all the problems and challenges that churches do. It was not perfect. But it had people from all over the world worshiping and serving Jesus Christ together! There were people in attendance from Indonesia, Russia, Scotland, Australia, China, France, Kenya, Haiti, Malaysia, the Philippines, America, New Zealand, India, Canada, and more. All these people were worshiping Christ together in the capital of the world's third largest democracy and the world's most populous Muslim country. Of course, Jennifer and I did not hesitate to say yes when the church offered the job. We could move before the year was over.

\* \* \* \* \*

The prospect of leaving Alabama and moving to Indonesia was exciting. God had given us another opportunity to serve outside the United States and an opportunity to "not waste" ourselves. With the Lord's help, we determined not to be like those people Dr. K had described at the Subway sandwich shop.

This was exciting, but there would be lots of details to manage. We needed to sell our house, our cars, our camper, and we would need to do something with most of our furniture. I would need to inform the church in Alabama that we were leaving (that would be painful) and we all needed passports along with a battery of vaccinations. We were confident though that every detail would fall into place. There was, however, one very large question on our minds: "Could an American family really adopt from Vietnam while moving to Indonesia?"

## CHAPTER SEVEN: NGO THI XAUN MAI

Mr. Tran Van Hoa sat in a bamboo chair inside the
security booth. It was good to rest after pacing about
the orphanage property for three hours. Although it
was only nine in the morning, he was already well
into his workday. He relaxed into the smell of his
hot breakfast noodles. He could almost sleep.
"What? Was that a baby crying? But the children are
in the courtyard with the nannies. Oh, it's outside
the gate!"

Rising from his chair, Mr. Hoa exited the back of his
post and then came around to the main orphanage
gate. He could hear a child crying outside. Taking
the key ring from his belt, he unlatched the padlock
and chain, which held the two halves of the iron gate
together. They swung apart, revealing a little girl.
She lay right on the sidewalk, crying and distressed.
Mr. Hoa picked her up. "Quiet, little girl," he
whispered. But she continued to moan. Tears ran
down her round cheeks.

Mr. Hoa took the little girl inside and quickly handed
her over to a surprised nanny. He was more

comfortable chasing off would-be thieves than he was holding little girls. However, he could not help being moved by the frightened look in her eyes.

The next day, he wrote his official report:

"My name is Tran Van Hoa. I work for the Care and Vocational Training Center as a security guard. In the morning, when I was on duty, I heard a child crying and rushed out to check. I found a child abandoned in the front gate of the center at No. 26 Ngo Quyen, Thang Nhat Ward, Vung Tau City. The abandoned child was a female infant. She has a full face, black eyes, flat nose, Asian skin; her hair was black and tied on top by elastic. She weighed about 10.5 kilograms. She was dressed in white clothing with a yellow hem. Besides that, there was no note or paper on her."

Mr. Hoa submitted his report in person to a small government committee, which was convened in the office of the orphanage where the child had been abandoned. The committee of two men and two women accepted the report and recommended the child be placed in the orphanage while a search was made for her parents. Since there was no information at all on the little girl, the committee followed established procedure assigning her a name and birth date. She was to be called Ngo Thi Xuan Mai. Ngo Thi helped identify the orphanage region and Xuan Mai after the name of a famous

Vietnamese singer. The committee set her date of birth at January 15, 2006.

For the next several days the government ran announcements in the local paper and on the radio, asking the parents of the child to come and claim her. If there were parents who heard these announcements, they did not or could not come forward. Ngo Thi Xuan Mai was now a ward of the Socialist Republic of Vietnam. What had happened to her parents was anybody's guess.

\* \* \* \* \*

For those of us who have regular employment and a place to live, it is easy to say we would never give up a child. However, we do not know what it is like to be homeless, jobless, and without any hope for your next meal while caring for a little child. For people in this situation, it may seem to them the most loving thing they can do for the child in their care (whether it is their own son or daughter or they are the guardian of someone else's child) is to hand him or her over to an organization that has some resources. It is not over-statement to say that the life of the child may be at stake.

I cannot imagine myself ever giving up one of my sons or daughters, but I refuse to judge those who have left their little ones on the doorsteps of orphanages, churches, and hospitals because they firmly believed they were saving their children. Probably we will never know what happened to the biological parents of Ngo Thi Xuan Mai. If one or more of them are still alive, then they may be among the tens of millions who thought leaving their child in the care of the state would save her life. I think such a heartbreaking sacrifice ought never to be despised.

The circumstances of Ngo Thi Xuan Mai's arrival outside the orphanage in Vung Tau remind us that every adoption story, however happily things turn out, begins in brokenness and pain. The good news of a successful adoption can only come on the heels of the bad news that something is wrong in this world. This sting does not go away on this side of eternity, and we should be prepared to help adopted children who feel the pain of it as they grow.

* * * * *

On September 12, 2007, around lunchtime, our phone rang. When Jennifer answered, she heard our attorney's voice saying, "You have been matched with a child for adoption! No family could be found for a little girl who was abandoned at an orphanage South of Saigon. Her name is Ngo Thi Xuan Mai."

Thanks to the wonders of the Internet, we were looking at a little picture of her within moments. She wore a white t-shirt and pink pants. Her black hair was pulled up and tied so it stuck straight up in the air on top of her head and she was clasping her little hands together in front. She had a very pretty face with dark eyes, but also wore an unhappy frown as if she was worrying over something. I remembered again that old coffee table book picture of the Vietnamese girl who needed help. Here was another, only with the Lord's help, we were going to rescue her!

We already had a name in mind for this little one. We chose the name Faith because of our hope that she would have faith in the Lord Jesus at the earliest possible age and because of our own trust in God's help bringing her into our family. Again and again we thought of this verse as we went through the adoption process:

"Now faith is the assurance of things hoped for, the conviction of things not seen" (Hebrews 11:1, ESV).

## CHAPTER EIGHT: DARK DAYS

After accepting the job in Indonesia, we informed our adoption professionals we were planning a big move. Their reaction was divided. Our Indiana lawyer was excited for us and eagerly accepted the challenge of throwing one more country into the mix. Our Alabama social worker, however, was appalled and declared such a move absolutely forbidden.

This was a perplexing situation for Jennifer and me. We have always been people who like to play by the rules. However, when the people making the rules disagreed, we were forced to decide for ourselves what our next step should be. We certainly sensed God calling us to Indonesia, but we also had no doubt it was his desire for us to adopt Faith from Vietnam. We decided to proceed cautiously at this point, informing the church in Jakarta of our desire to complete the adoption before we moved, while at the same time putting our house on the market to sell and breaking the news to North Hills Church that our days in Alabama were numbered. Since we had already been matched with a child, we anticipated the possibility of completing the adoption before the year was over and arriving in Jakarta in time for the Christmas season.

To our surprise, we sold our home almost immediately. Our close friends from Church, Aaron and Erica Hammond (who were in the process of adopting from China) wanted to buy the place. This was great news because it would help us get out of debt and free from the mortgage. Within a month we had closed the deal, signed the papers, and we were packing up to move out. Just up the road from North Hills Church, there was an old church manse which was unused by the Cumberland Presbyterians. They agreed to let our family stay there for two or three months. The house itself was small, just three bedrooms, and was last decorated around 1970. Nevertheless, the location was great and we were thankful for its availability.

\* \* \* \* \*

Joshua, Andrew, and I were unloading the last round of boxes from the back of the 35-foot U-Haul truck. A large stack was growing in the garage of the Seventies House (our nickname for the old manse). We staggered, with boxes in our hands, up and down the ramp that stretched from the truck into the cold garage. It was 10 PM and this would be our last run between the house we had just sold and our temporary dwelling. Tomorrow, we would no longer be in our own home. Rather than being nervous or sad, it was kind of a thrill. We all knew we were making a move for the Lord.

I was so proud of Joshua and Andrew. Over the previous weeks, the two boys had worked like grown men, packing things up at home. We had also cleared out the garage, cleaned up the attic, managed garage sales, and for the past 12 hours we had been using the U-Haul to deposit furniture in storage. After breakfast the next day, the house was to be empty for our friends the Hammonds. There were just a couple dozen boxes with items for Jakarta that needed to go into the temporary garage. We were almost finished. Tired as I was, I could see the light at the end of the tunnel. That was, however, until the phone rang.

"Hello?" I answered after fumbling at the phone buttons with my cold fingers.

"Stop unloading the truck!" It was Jennifer.

"Why? What do you mean? We're almost done!"

"I just got a call from our social worker. She said we're not allowed to move out of our house. It will ruin our home study and we won't be able to continue the adoption!"

"She called you at this time of night to tell you this?"

"Yes, I think she must have read that we were moving on our blog. She says we cannot move into the seventies house. It is way too small and would never pass the home study inspection. She is really upset!"

"She's upset?" I muttered. "Stop boys, stop!" I commanded with little sensitivity. "I need to think just a minute."

Jennifer was silent on the line while we both pondered our situation. We could not move out of our house, but we also could not stay there, because it really was not our house anymore and the new owner was coming the next day. In fact, they were loading their own U-Haul that very night. Our home was gone and we could not go to another. I cannot really describe the way I felt about this. It was crushing. Not only was I uncertain about where our family would sleep the next evening, I had this great fear we had ruined our chance of getting Faith from Vietnam. Not to mention that some people thought we were absolutely nuts already. "Wait until they hear about this!" I thought aloud. "I'm coming home," I told Jennifer, "and we can talk some more. Love you."

The boys and I did finish emptying the truck because it needed to go back to the rental place in the morning. Then we closed the garage and drove home. We were all confused and depressed. Good thing we did not know that later that night, thieves would break into the seventies house and steal some of our valuables.

* * * * *

Late that night, Jennifer telephoned our friends, Aaron and Erica, to tell them what our social worker had said. To our great encouragement, they immediately offered to delay their move while we tried to figure out what to do. I will never forget the Christian love they showed us in doing this. It meant they had to store most of their belongings in our garage (which was really their garage) and then move in with relatives. They put some of their own furniture in the house so we could use it, since ours had already been stored away. Although I joked about how they would become our former friends after we put them in this awkward spot, they never once indicated that it was anything other than their joy to help us. Praise God for Christian people like them!

The morning after we received the dreaded call, I was on the phone with our social worker trying to figure something out. The bottom line was, she was unbendable on two points. First, if we moved out of our current home, then we would need to have our home study updated to reflect our new status. Second, the home we moved into would need to be at least as big and new as our current house (or former house depending on your perspective). After we politely wrapped up that conversation, I telephoned our adoption attorney, Michele Jackson, in Indiana. Her analysis of the situation seemed a little more hopeful. The home study was completed, it had been handed over to the government of Vietnam and US Citizenship Services, and we had been matched with a child. The governments would not ask for a home study update before the adoption was completed. However, Michele was very level-headed and hoped we could work things out to everyone's satisfaction, including our social worker in Alabama.

Once again, Jennifer and I found ourselves in a situation where the expert professionals were advising us differently. Obviously, we favored the counsel of our lawyer, but we did not wish to be adoptive renegades or anything like that. We truly wanted to do things in the most forthright and proper manner.

With the information we had, we decided to take the following course of action: We would rent the biggest, newest, cheapest, temporary home we could find. This way we would be in compliance with the spirit of the instructions given by our social worker. However, we knew we could not afford to have our home study updated. It would be very costly (we were nearly broke by this point) and we felt our process was near the end. So, we determined to be ready for a home study update by getting the proper house, but to wait (if we could) as long as possible. In other words, we were going to stall and hope the process would be completed before it was necessary to make any changes.

This was not the most comfortable approach for me, but Jennifer and I felt it was up to us to prayerfully do what we thought was best. God forgive us if we were wrong. However, this was not to be the last time we would be forced to make an unorthodox move in our adoption journey.

We found a huge (and I mean gigantic) house for rent, which was not too far from work. It was in a new neighborhood and seemed to be a place that would comply with any size and safety standards. It was also somewhat within our grasp financially. To us, finding this place was an affirmation of our plans. We settled in the new house in October, with the hope that we could leave there shortly after the adoption was completed.

During our first week at the latest house, we made quite an impression on the neighbors. I had brought over a few pieces of furniture for us and some toys and games for our kids. There was a cavernous room upstairs in the temporary place where we set up an old skee-ball table. One afternoon during our first week in the neighborhood, three-year-old Grace somehow got her finger stuck in a small hole on the side of this table. Our best efforts to get her finger out proved fruitless. We tried lotion, oil, and soap. All the while, her cute little finger continued to swell up and change colors from pink, to red, to purple. In frustration we decided to call our pediatrician and ask him if he had any suggestions.

After we described the situation to him, he immediately recommended we dial 911 for emergency assistance. "You have got to be kidding!" I thought. "How could such a small little thing become such a big deal?" Nevertheless, I did not have any better ideas so I punched in that important combination of numbers and reported my emergency to the operator. Apparently, there was not an ambulance available, so they sent out the closest emergency vehicle, which happened to be a huge fire truck. It pulled up in front with lights flashing and sirens blaring.

Moments later, we had six firefighters gathered around little Grace. By this time her finger was swollen to an epic proportion, but she was calmly sitting on a little kid chair and sucking on a lollipop. The firefighters tried many of the same things we had already tried with the same lack of success. They decided they needed something to cut the table so her finger could be released. Unfortunately, they did not have the tools they wanted on their truck, so they decided to call another. Moments later, a second truck roared up with its own dramatic sirens and lights. As another bunch of firefighters were making their way up the stairs to the skee-ball room, one final emergency vehicle pulled up. This was an ambulance, which soon dispensed a couple more rescue personnel into our new temporary house.

Glancing out onto the street I could see a row of emergency equipment at the curb in front of the house with lights still strobing and flashing. Neighbors had moved onto their lawns with looks of great concern for the obviously terrible thing that must have happened to the new people on the block. Turning away from the window I saw about 15 tough looking firefighters and paramedics gathered in a circle around a little girl in a pink dress who sat calmly enjoying her cherry lollipop. I really wanted to take a picture of this but decided that would be tacky. One of our teenagers did, however, get a photo of the trucks on our street.

The firefighters decided to use a large reciprocating saw to cut the table up to where Grace's finger was stuck. This was scary because it meant the fast-moving metal blade would go up right next to her finger. This course of action greatly disturbed one ambulance paramedic, but she could not talk the others out of proceeding accordingly. It was then that she did something which made all this craziness seem worth it to me. Announcing in her thick Alabama accent, "I don't like this at all ya'll," she then wrapped her own hand around our little girl's finger and said, "Honey, I will not let this saw hurt you."

I was very impressed. It was a beautiful gesture of love and reminded me of our Savior Jesus, who placed his own body on the cross to save and protect us from sin and death. What a great world we would live in if more people showed this kind of Christ-like love to needy little ones!

The sawing was a success and neither Grace nor the loving paramedic were injured. The game was broken for good, our daughter was free, we thanked the rescue teams as they climbed back into their trucks, and we headed over to meet the neighbors.

\* \* \* \* \*

It was right about this time that a new problem made its way to the surface. We were totally broke. To be fair, I must say how amazed I had been up to this point by the way the Lord had provided for us financially. Friends and family had given us financial gifts; we received a grant from our church, and we even got a gift from Show Hope, an organization founded by Steven Curtis and Mary Beth Chapman in 2003 with a mission to care for orphans by reducing the barriers to adoption. This money passed through our hands, and with thankfulness to God, we gave it to our adoption agency, our lawyer, and numerous government departments in America and Vietnam. However, by October 2007, everything seemed to dry up, including my faith that God would provide.

Although some people thought we were crazy, I was not ashamed of looking foolish for trying to adopt an orphan or for trying to leave a comfortable ministry in America for an uncertain future in Indonesia. Our hearts' desire in doing these things was to be within the will of God. That being the case, it did not matter what anyone else in the universe thought about it. But I was no saint in the process, that's for sure. I am ashamed of my lack of trust in the Lord to provide the finances we needed for the adoption. I remembered my comment to Jennifer the year before when we got our first estimate on how much the adoption would cost. "I'll worry about the money," I had said. And indeed, I did worry about it!

I applied for every adoption grant and loan I could find. This is not an exaggeration. I went down the list of options for financial assistance that we were given by our adoption agency and contacted every single one (except for the one that was only for Jewish people). I surfed the Internet for other options and when I found them, I contacted them too. This was not an entirely fruitless exercise. It resulted in the gracious gift from Steven Curtis Chapman's foundation and later would produce a zero-interest loan from the Abba Fund. However, most of these attempts were dead ends. A couple of groups replied that our family had been approved for a grant. Unfortunately, they were out of money at the moment. Well, I supposed, it is the thought that counts.

I went to my local bank to apply for a personal loan. This was the same bank that had cheerfully loaned me the money to buy the Suburban and camper. Suddenly, however, they thought I was too great a risk. In fact, the loan officer practically threw me out of her office. Meanwhile, the adoption bills kept pouring in. We had passed the original $17,000 estimate long before October 2007 and there did not appear to be an end in sight.

This should have been the time that I cast myself before God and placed my total trust and confidence in him. Jennifer was. She really was certain that the Lord could provide every penny. I, on the other hand, was scared. I do not know for sure why. Perhaps it was the shock of the night we were told we could not move from our house after we had just sold it to someone else. I imagined a situation where we would be told we could not adopt Faith because we could not pay. So instead of praying and asking

God for wisdom and help to meet this need, I went to a high rate private loan company and took out a loan. These nice guys also gave me a credit card with a huge limit. "I'm still trusting God," I told myself. "This is just in case." But I knew it wasn't true. I do not think it is wrong to borrow money for an adoption. It's just that, for me, I was pretending to trust God while really looking to CitiFinancial for help.

The proof that my heart was not right is that I said nothing about this to Jennifer. I rationalized that was good. After all, I had promised her I would worry about the money. She would work on the paperwork; I would work on the money. That was the deal. I even tried to convince myself I was protecting her from the stress and doing her a favor by not letting her in on all this. She had plenty of other things on her plate as it was. To some, this may seem like no big deal. However, Jennifer and I have always shared everything. We make our decisions together, we relate all the details of each day with one another, and we are best friends. During this time, whenever we prayed about the money we needed for the adoption, I felt a kind of separation from her, and from God too.

Three months went by before I told her about this. She forgave me, but from that point I felt more dependent on our creditors for funds than on the

Lord Jesus. Looking back, I really regret that. It is the biggest thing in our adoption journey that I wish I had done differently.

\* \* \* \* \*

That is not to say we were not trusting God for many other things. He made sure we had to! Somewhere between the US immigration offices (USCIS) and the government agency that handled adoptions in Vietnam, there was a problem. I still do not completely understand what the issue was, but somehow these two government bodies were not communicating with each other and all forward progress on Faith's adoption came to a screeching halt. Although we thought we would be getting a call to travel to Vietnam any day, October passed, then November. We celebrated Thanksgiving in the temporary house, then Christmas. On New Year's Eve, we received word from Vietnam that it might be months longer. In fact, the Vietnam adoption program was under a lot of scrutiny and might even be completely shut down.

This was very discouraging and a big problem. I had already contacted the church in Jakarta and moved the time we intended to arrive on the field twice. Likewise, I had twice asked my current employer if they would let me stay a little longer. Meanwhile, the lease on the big house we were staying in would soon be up. Not to mention our home study situation and many of our government documents already had to be renewed. These renewals cost lots of money, thus driving the price of the adoption into the stratosphere!

Jennifer and I were at our wits end. We could not leave the house we were renting, but we could not stay in the house, either. We could not leave my job at North Hills Church, but we could not keep extending my time there. We could not leave the country, but we could not pass up on the opportunity to relocate to Jakarta. We absolutely would not give up on adopting Faith, but there were no guarantees and there was no timetable.

I remember that New Year's holiday well. My dear parents were there. As we explained our situation, they offered many ideas. Although their suggestions were good, I can remember explaining how each alternative did not work. It was a discouraging process for us all. Jennifer and I had to retreat to our bedroom and try to gather our thoughts. We were supposed to be in a festive mood, but we were beginning to slide into a crazy depression.

The Lord was with us, however, and we decided to pray. I remember sitting together and telling God we had absolutely no clue what our next move should be. None of our choices were good ones. Together Jennifer and I begged God to help us. We did not even know what to ask Him for, but we pleaded for mercy in Jesus' Name. When we got up from our prayer, we felt at peace. However, we still had no answers. We were resigned to whatever God would do.

# CHAPTER NINE: IN INDONESIA

Jennifer and I did not doubt the Lord had placed a double calling in our lives. We were confident that He wanted us to adopt little Faith Xuan Mai from Vietnam. How could we doubt this for an instant? The Lord had declared that, "pure religion is this: to look after... orphans in their distress" (James 1:27). We were also confident that He was calling us to serve Him in Jakarta. "Go to all nations and preach the gospel" (Mark 16:15). It was strange that these two callings from God appeared to be conflicting in our current circumstances, but it seemed that either would be easier without the other.

The pressure was mounting as we entered the New Year, 2008. It did not seem wise to continue "in limbo" as we were. Jennifer and I determined it was time to make a decision. Thinking logically, it was easier than expected. On the one hand, the adoption situation was not making any apparent forward progress. Although we felt confident the Lord would work things out positively in the end, there was no indication at all of how long it would take.

On the other hand, we could begin the ministry in Jakarta as soon as we were ready.

After another round of talks with our lawyer, we were once again ready to make an unorthodox judgment call. Prayerfully, we determined to move to Jakarta and attempt completing the adoption from there. This was risky because we were not 100 percent certain it was even allowable, but we had passed our comfort zone long before and trusted that God would "work all things together for our good."

However, there was another catch to our plan. We decided there was no way we could fly all eight of us to Vietnam to pick up Faith when the time came. Furthermore, we were not comfortable with the thought of leaving several of our children behind in Jakarta with new friends for three weeks while Jennifer and I went alone to Vietnam. Our solution to this problem was to leave four of the six children in America while we moved over to Asia. This way, Jennifer and I could travel with just two of the kids to Vietnam and pick up Faith. Once we had her, then the others could fly over and join us in Indonesia.

This would probably be a good place to back up and say a little more about the role our six children played in our adoption and move. Many people have asked us, "What do the other kids think about the adoption? Are they okay with it?" These are always strange questions for us to hear because adoption was something we all pursued together. Jennifer and I never felt that we were forcing this on our kids. On the contrary; they prayed many times each day for Faith, they picked out presents for her, drew pictures for her, imagined what it would be like to have her with us, and just generally encouraged their mom and dad all along the way. The adoption was a team effort on the part of each member in our family. I am so thankful for this. Rather than driving our family apart, as many suppose, adoption only brought us closer together.

Likewise, the kids were supportive of serving the Lord on the mission field. When I was in Jakarta interviewing for the position at the church, Jennifer asked seven-year-old Simon Peter, "What would you think if God called your daddy to be a missionary in Indonesia?"

Simon answered, "I would miss him, but if that is what God wants, then that is okay."

Thankfully, Jennifer could tell Simon we would all go together! Still, his answer was a sweet blessing to me and evidence that God can work in the hearts of the very young, not only so they may be saved through faith, but also so they can sacrifice for the kingdom and serve the Lord their God.

\* \* \* \* \*

The result of our decision to move was a wild round of communication with new friends in Jakarta, heart rending goodbyes with old friends in Alabama, more packing, tons of paperwork for visas, and at last the loading of an ocean container with items for setting up our household in Indonesia.

With all of this done, our departure was one day away. On February 10, 2008, Jennifer's parents arrived to help us clean up the few things that were left in the big temporary house. The social worker for whom we rented the place had never seen it and so far as I know still knows nothing about it. It was also Simon Peter's eighth birthday. I was exceedingly sad because I knew the next day I would leave him and his brothers Andrew, Jacob, and Elijah behind for an uncertain amount of time. We liked to say it would be a month or less, but the truth is we had no way of really knowing. Past performance did not bode well for the future.

That night we moved out of the house and went to a hotel. Simon's birthday party was in an Asian restaurant, and then we played at the hotel pool. His grandparents had bought him a nice pair of Crocs, but we had nothing to give him since everything was packed up and we were headed out for the airport in the morning. I felt like a real loser. As I sat on the side of the pool, Simon came up and said, "Daddy, is this a no-present birthday?" I wanted to just burst into tears right then, but I explained to Simon that things were kind of strange right now and we were all having a good time together in the pool. He seemed convinced, but I was not. Simon and his brothers comfort me now by saying he celebrated his birthday at least three more times that year while he stayed with two sets of grandparents and his uncle. However, it still hurts when I remember that day. It's one thing to talk about making sacrifices in order to follow God's leading, but quite another thing to begin feeling the pinch.

Having said that, I think those of us who are called to serve the Lord in ministry must be careful to remain focused on the responsibility we have to our children. I cannot blame the Lord for my own lack of sensitivity and distraction from the people in my life who matter most. When we are involved in adoption ministry, missions, or pastoring, the work is always important and often feels urgent. Nevertheless, God has called us to minister to our families first. I wish I had worked harder to stay more focused on how each child was doing, even during those busy days.

The next morning, we all gathered around to say goodbye. It was hard for us to leave Jennifer's dear parents, Jamie and Doug, but the greatest emotional rending centered on the four boys who would be staying behind. I looked at my son Andrew, 13 at the time, and said to him, "Now, you will lay down your life for these little ones, right?"

"Yes, sir," he said. And I could tell he meant it too. It was a very dear moment for me as his daddy, and I have often thought about it. Andrew had always been quiet and reserved, but something changed in him when we left. Ironically, I was afraid he would be somehow scarred by the experience. Instead, however, he became so thoughtful, responsible, and serious about caring for his family that he continues to set a good example for me. I am amazed and thankful for the grace and strength God gave.

But everything was uncertain in those moments when we said goodbye. After praying, hugging, crying, and going through the painful process of separation, Jennifer, Joshua, Grace, and I drove away in a rented van. We were headed to Atlanta where we would catch our plane. Jennifer and I had decided to take our oldest, because he could be most helpful on our journey, and our youngest, because she was the baby and only girl at the time. We felt numb but slowly came to life as we realized we were about to begin a great adventure.

\* \* \* \* \*

On February 14, 2008, we landed in balmy Jakarta, Indonesia. Our first weeks in the Indonesian capital are still a blur in my mind. When I look at pictures from that time, it feels like I am seeing someone else. Part of this was the jet lag, part of it was cultural adjustment, and perhaps some was just good old-fashioned stress. It was not that we were unhappy with the church or Jakarta. In fact, both were very exciting to us. Even when there were challenges, we could rejoice that God had placed us in so great a city and in a strategic ministry among people from all over the world.

Having said that, the challenges were real!

One of the cultural surprises we faced in Indonesia was the expectation that we would have a household staff. In fact, the staff came with our first house like kitchen fixtures might be included in an American home. We had a maid, cook, driver, and gardener who, along with their children, lived with us during most of our time in Jakarta. Any thought of doing without these workers was set aside by the reality that they desperately needed the money and a place to live. It was simply standard for foreigners and wealthy Indonesians to provide employment for others.

I know it is difficult for Americans to feel sorry for us on this point, and I must admit I enjoyed having someone else shop, cook my dinner, clean the house, and navigate the horrid traffic of our town. Having said that, it was difficult to relax in our Indonesian homes. We were rarely, if ever, alone, and felt the burden of responsibility to provide healthcare, education, and wise counsel for these poor families. Furthermore, they were all Muslim. I was glad for that in a way because it gave us the opportunity to share Christ as we were able. On the other hand, they were (at least socially and politically) faithful practitioners of their faith and expected we would be supportive of that. This led to some occasional awkward circumstances, such as when we insisted that our driver work during his prayer time or when we were obligated to pay for some Islamic ritual. We did our best to get it right, to support our Muslim employees while honoring Christ. It was not always easy.

There were times, however, when our Muslim friends proved themselves dear to us. Such as when my driver noticed I was waiting outside in the sun for an appointment and came and stood with me, holding an umbrella. Our gardener chopped open coconuts, so the kids could drink the milk and our cook chased away people who might have taken advantage of us. On occasion, they showed great bravery. During our first year in Jakarta, the stove in our home caught on fire. It was a propane stove with the propane tank built inside. Our cook announced there was a fire and we all fled the house. Then she and the other workers all marched back inside. I followed, planning to order them all back out to safety.

By this point, the propane gas tank was completely engulfed. When I entered the kitchen, the men were taking turns running across the room and throwing buckets of water or wet towels onto the tank. I was using my broken Indonesian to encourage them all to leave. It was not worth the risk, I told them. There were numerous news reports of propane tanks blowing up in Jakarta. The situation was truly terrifying. It felt there could be an explosion any second. The house helpers continued to ignore me and fight the fire. Suddenly, the gardener and guard from the house next door came over to assist. It was then that I realized how out of touch I was. There was no fire department here.

The houses were all within a few feet of each other. There were 14 people living in our small house. More lived in the homes adjacent to us. If the tank blew, people all around would lose their few possessions, and some could be killed. No one was coming to help. We had to put it out ourselves. After about 10 minutes, the fire was suffocated in wet towels and blankets. We were safe. I did not help, but stood there the whole time, ashamed to obey my instinct to run off. The household staff simply started cleaning up.

We did not often feel in danger living in Jakarta. You simply get used to things. Hotels we visited were bombed (thankfully not while we were there), we were in an earthquake, we drove in insane traffic in the city and the countryside, we visited the inside of an active volcano, and we occasionally passed through rioting mobs. I had apparently demon possessed people call down curses upon me and one local business person threaten me with murder. One of our staff attempted suicide at our home. Jennifer suffered from a mysterious long-term illness. Somehow, though, it felt like normal life in Southeast Asia.

There were positive events as well. On one occasion, a man took me to lunch in a café after he visited our church. He told me that when he came into church that Sunday, he was planning to kill his wife. I thought he was joking, but he did not crack a smile. He had really meant it. The family was broken when the wife ran off with another man and took her young son with her. The boy was hidden away in a Muslim boarding school. Using private security personal, my new friend had managed to get his child back, but he was seeking revenge on his ex-wife. He told me, however, that something about the gospel he heard in our church stopped him in his tracks. This man became a good friend and a dear Christian brother. He and his son were baptized in our swimming pool. He was changed from a man contemplating murder to a kind Christian father. When I last saw him, he was speaking about ways he might try to assist his ex-wife with her personal problems.

On another occasion, three individuals from a closed Muslim country entered our church on Sunday morning and attended the Sunday school class I was teaching. When we went around the room and introduced ourselves, the more outgoing of the group announced, "We are here to change our religion." Shame on me, because I did not really want to delve into that just then and suggested we speak after class. Afterwards, the three approached me and again the man said, "We want to change our religion. We were beaten in our home country for watching American movies. We realize that Islam is always about rules and there is a cruel harshness. We see in Christ, there is freedom." This was a compelling statement and I did want to hear more, but it was time for me to head into the worship service where I would be preaching. I put them off again, suggesting that we could talk after church.

When the service ended, the three visitors could wait on me no longer. Instead they approached my friend and assistant pastor Dave Atkins, pretty much demanding to be told about Jesus. Dave shared the gospel message with the two men and one woman. The three confessed their sins and trusted Jesus right there on the spot. The next day, Pastor Dave baptized them in the swimming pool at our house. The three were presented with Bibles after their baptisms. It was amazing to see their faces light up as they held the word of God in their hands for the first time. Later, we learned that one of the three returned to his home country as an undercover missionary. I have often thought about how I missed the blessing of leading these middle-easterners to Christ because I was too busy doing ministry. There is a life lesson there for sure.

I am so grateful that our children were able to witness those baptisms. They were seeing the power of Christ at work in the transformation of lives. These experiences make a big impact. Eleven-year-old Jacob was so inspired by the effectiveness of the good news that he felt God was calling him to head out and share it right away. One night, while we all slept, he slipped through the gate of our property and onto the streets of Jakarta. In his childlike way, he truly felt compelled to head out and share Jesus with some needy Indonesians.

Of course, from our adult point of view, this was a poor (and terrifying) choice. As he wandered the streets in the dark, he came across a kind Indonesian man who suggested he had no business on the street at night and escorted him home. If you know these Asian mega-cities, then you know the outcome could have been very different. I think this man may have been an angel of God sent to take care of our boy. To be fair to Jacob, he has kept his heart for the lost and is now studying in college with the goal of becoming a missionary. His childish heart may have been foolish back then, but on the other hand our Lord Jesus applauds this sort of faith saying, "The kingdom of heaven belongs to such as these" (Mark 10:14b).

All the children made some sacrifices to live in Indonesia. We moved three times during our four years there. The second two houses were spacious, but the first was tiny. The five brothers shared a small bedroom together and there were only four beds. Our youngest son Elijah slept on a floor mat for an entire year. Through all that, he never complained. He was just happy to be with his family, where God wanted him to be.

There were opportunities to serve outside of our church ministry as well. One of our favorites was visiting Bukit Karmel orphanage in the countryside of Java. Founded years ago, by an inspiring Australian Christian woman, this place was home for several dozen orphans. We would travel over occasionally and try to help with the work there. We partnered with some Christian friends in repairing and repainting the buildings, but the work we enjoyed most was simply spending time with the kids. Joshua and Andrew would play with the big kids while the rest of us went into the nursery to help there.

The nursery housed about a dozen babies. The orphanage staff went above and beyond to care for these little ones, but there were never enough hands to provide the physical love and contact they needed. Our task was simple. We held babies, gave them bottles, and changed diapers. Children who start life in an institution grow up without the human touch and contact needed for positive adjustment and attachment to others. Appropriate physical contact helps them feel more secure in the world.

Among the residents of the nursery was a boy named Kevin. Kevin had hydrocephalus (also known as water on the brain). His condition was obvious from his slow development and even his physical appearance. Although he was over a year old, he normally lay on the floor mat like a newborn. Kevin also had a heart condition and a hernia. The hernia was not a particularly serious medical issue, but the other problems presented such serious complications that the doctors could not proceed with the simple hernia operation. All that could be done was to pray for this little orphan and many prayers were offered by the director, staff, and friends of the orphanage.

After several weeks of specific prayer for Kevin, he was taken to the city for a check-up. The doctor who examined him was amazed to find the hernia was gone! Further examination revealed that his heart condition was corrected and, most amazingly, the hydrocephalus was no longer present. From a medical point of view all of this was astonishing! Though I believe God can heal (and obviously does), I have not been close to many stories like this. Nevertheless, there Kevin was, back in the nursery, improving daily and even looking different. It is one of the most astonishing medical miracles I have encountered. It is a reminder that even when it seems no one else cares, the God of the universe is looking out for the weak and needy in this world. He is their great Heavenly Father, Defender, and Healer. We saw him at work in many ways during our time in Indonesia.

Rolling the clock back to those first few weeks, though, we were busy learning to live in our new situation at the church and at home. We made time to call America via Skype and talk with the boys nearly every day. Praise God for this technology. Years before, when we stayed in Madagascar, it was as if we had dropped off the face of the earth. Back then, we would send letters and hope they made it weeks later. Today, however, the Internet has really made living internationally much easier. Along with contacting the kids, technology was also useful for contacting our adoption attorney. We were constantly working to make sure everything was ready for us to travel to Vietnam as soon as we heard the word "go." It seemed, however, that the process was going nowhere. We prayed, "How long, Oh Lord?"

## CHAPTER TEN: IN VIETNAM AT LAST

On March 26, 2008, the email we had been waiting for finally arrived! It indicated that we had an I-600 approval by the United States Immigration Agency. This meant we were cleared to take Faith from Vietnam. I bought the tickets that same day using a credit card, because we only had enough cash to pay the in-country expenses when we got to Vietnam. We gave no thought at all to the cost. There was nothing that was going to stand in our way at this point.

It had only been a little over two years since we began our adoption journey, but in a way it felt like forever. Suddenly the idea of heading over to get Faith seemed surreal and strange. We were happy and excited, but also felt numbed by the whole experience. Our entire family had invested so much of ourselves in this project I wondered if we had enough stamina to finish the race.

There was not much time to wonder, because we were soon on a plane headed to Ho Chi Minh City (Saigon). Jennifer, Joshua, Grace, and I were trying our best to act relaxed like a family headed off on vacation. We knew we would see another country, stay in hotels, eat meals out, and most importantly add another member to our family! However, our celebratory mood was slightly dampened by the stress of the previous months and the uncertainty of how things might go on the ground in Vietnam. But ready or not, we soon found ourselves staggering down the ramp into the Saigon Airport.

We were met by an aged Vietnamese man named Tom and his daughter. Tom had been hired by the Vietnamese government to serve as our translator. Apparently, he brought his daughter along to translate for him. Throughout our time in Saigon, we had these two along with us. Conversation would often flow from us to the daughter to Tom and then to anyone we wanted to speak with. Then it would flow back through Tom to the daughter and then to us. This seemed an odd way, but we assumed since we were their guests we would just go with it.

Our translators took us by taxi across town to a hotel. Once they had us checked in, we were told to stay in the room and wait for a message. One hour turned into two and then into three. The four of us stared out the window at the busy street below. Perhaps Vietnam would have seemed more exotic if we had not recently moved to Jakarta. There seemed (at least to us green Americans) to be many similarities between the two countries. The roads were choked with motorbikes and people of all ages swarmed up and down the sidewalks doing business, visiting friends, playing games, or just hanging out. After a while of waiting, I headed down to the desk and asked if there was a message for me. In broken English, the clerk said, "Tomorrow."

"Tomorrow?" I repeated.

"Tomorrow," she said again.

"But, it sounded like I would get a message here today?"

"Tomorrow," she said a third time.

"Okay," I answered while turning away to find the elevator back up. "Seems like everyone knows what is going on except for me."

Jennifer, the two kids, and I went out to look for some dinner. We began to notice at least one difference between Vietnam and Indonesia. We could not find any western food chains in Saigon. It seemed all the restaurant choices were geared toward the locals and too overwhelming for tired foreigners like us. However, as we wandered the city streets, we did eventually stumble across a bit of a surprise, a Brazilian Restaurant. After eating more meat than we had seen in the past year, we made our way back into the hotel and soon were fast asleep.

\* \* \* \* \*

Tomorrow came early with a call from the front desk announcing the arrival of Tom, his daughter, and our lawyer's agent, a young woman named Anna. Anna's English was perfect. When I asked her where she had studied English, she said she learned it from watching American movies. We traveled to a few government offices so we could complete some paperwork for the adoption and Anna gave us the good news that we would make the two-hour drive south to Vung Tau and pick up our new daughter the next day!

We will never forget March 31, 2008. We were out of bed by 4:45 to start getting ready. After showering and dressing, we went up for breakfast at the Hotel Restaurant. Returning to our room, we gathered our things and headed down to the lobby. Tom and his ever-present daughter were already waiting on us. We went out and loaded into a van for the ride to Faith's orphanage. In the van, we met the driver and one other woman, who was a Vietnamese government worker.

The ride south was relatively uneventful. Poor little Gracie did get carsick for a while, but soon felt better. We drove past many shops and then the buildings thinned out while we rode on a developed highway, heading south through the rice fields. Vung Tau, the city in or near where Faith was most likely born, was a pretty little ocean town about two hours from the hotel. It had long been a beach resort for people who wanted to get out of Saigon for some fresh air. Interestingly, Vung Tau is home to a 91-foot-tall statue of Jesus that sits on a hill overlooking the beaches.

We pulled up at the orphanage around 10:30 AM. After walking through green steel gates, we entered a courtyard on the lower level and were asked to wait there for an invitation to go upstairs. The courtyard center was paved with polished stones and there were a few pieces of colorful playground equipment in the grass on the perimeter. Children were playing here and there. When they noticed us, some would smile and wave, others would look away. It quickly became obvious to us that this was not the same facility in the background of pictures we had seen of Faith. Later, we learned they moved the children just prior to the arrival of their adoptive parents. Perhaps this is because some facilities are nicer than others and they want to make a good impression if they can. I do not think this means they are trying to "get away" with anything. Who doesn't want to look their best for company?

After a few minutes, we were ushered up a set of metal stairs, across a balcony, and into the orphanage director's office. Here we met the director, a woman about our age. We sat down at a table together and began working on a stack of paperwork. We also had brought presents for the nannies, the orphanage director, and a customary financial gift for the orphanage. I remember hoping the money would really find its way into the operating budget of the place. The many official looking papers we signed that indicated the money was for that purpose pleased me. It also became apparent that the government lady who rode down with us was there to ensure the legality of the process as she stared over our shoulders and kept a watchful eye on all the proceedings.

I knew the adoption program in Vietnam was under a lot of scrutiny. In fact, shortly after we completed our adoption, the program was shut down. However, everything we observed in our process was transparent and legal. We had seen official corruption in other countries and never felt that we saw it in our adoption process. There were multiple copies of everything signed by many different officials, and we traveled to several government offices while in country. Vietnamese and US officials repeatedly reviewed the files. I understand children are stolen and abused in this world, but I think it would be a terrible thing if we used that sad reality as an excuse to leave orphans in institutions when they could become part of loving families.

While we were sitting in plastic chairs at a round wooden table, still in the process of signing papers, they brought Faith into the room without any special announcement. It was not anti-climactic, but it was as if she just appeared from nowhere. She wore a little pink and white outfit and her hair was tied up in two pigtails. She seemed nervous, but her face was mostly expressionless as she eyed the white people in the room.

Words cannot adequately express what the moment was like. We had been praying for this little girl for so long, it was hard to believe she was there and soon was in her new mother's arms. We kissed her, hugged her, told her we loved her, and praised God for her! Grace seemed happy to meet her new sister and Joshua was busily snapping photos. The moment we had been yearning for did not last long, because Tom was reminding us we still had many papers to sign.

Once the paperwork was complete, the orphanage director took us to a room where orphans were housed. It was a clean, but crowded, bunkroom. There were several children in the room, sitting on beds or just standing around. We were also taken to the baby nursery. We took a lot of pictures in the nursery because we knew an American couple that was planning to adopt a baby from Vung Tau. We were hoping that we could get a picture of her. After walking through these rooms, we were told it was time to go. All this time Faith had been quiet in her new mother's arms. There was no tearful farewell when she left the orphanage, but she did cry when we climbed into the van. The government lady, who apparently was still going to travel with us, explained that Faith had only ridden in a vehicle a few times and that was for doctor appointments.

We drove to a nearby government office where we signed more papers. I honestly had no clue what was going on or what we were signing. The overall experience was emotionally overwhelming, making it difficult to concentrate. Apparently, this was a significant stop, because it ended with a ceremonial photo shoot in front of a red curtain and a bust of Ho Chi Minh. Tom, via his daughter, announced that we were done. Faith was officially our daughter! The whole "gotcha" process had taken a little over one hour. Our new Vietnamese friends took us to a restaurant on the beach, where the girls played in the surf. When it was time to eat, Faith sat in Jennifer's lap and devoured anything and everything that we put in front of her.

After lunch, we drove back to Saigon. The ride was uneventful. Faith slept in Jennifer's arms almost the whole way while we all stared at her with amazement. We observed that her little body was covered with scars from scabies, which she had picked up at the orphanage. Joshua took lots of pictures of those scars. I remember being upset with him for doing that. Now, however, I like to see the pictures because most of the scars are gone!

As soon as we arrived back in Saigon, we were encouraged to switch hotels because space had become available at a better location in the heart of the tourist district. We complied and were glad we did since the next few days would involve little more than waiting for the next step in the adoption process. This gave us time at the hotel getting to know Faith and out on the town getting to know Vietnam.

\* \* \* \* \*

The Royal Kim Do Hotel became our home for two of the three weeks we were in Vietnam. It was an aging yet elegant facility right in the center of town. Once settled in our new rooms, we headed to the hotel dining room for dinner. We were the only people dining at the buffet and we enjoyed the undivided, overwhelming attention of the large wait staff.

Faith's eyes bulged as she saw the food on the table and she began stuffing things in her little mouth as fast as she could. It was neat to see her enjoying a variety of foods, at least until she filled up and overflowed. Our little Xaun Mai ate until she literally threw up. Interestingly, the waiters were over in a jiffy and went right to work cleaning her, the high chair, the table, and floor as quickly as they could. It was a humbling experience and we were grateful for their care. With that done, Faith was ready to eat some more. Appetite was not a problem for her. Moderation would continue to be a challenge for several months. Apparently, her little life experience had taught her that if you see some food, you had better eat it. In her short life, she had never felt guaranteed another meal.

\* \* \* \* \*

Bonding with a child who had been abandoned at an orphanage is not an easy matter. Faith quickly latched onto Jennifer and did not want to let her go. She eyed Jennifer the whole time we were in our hotel room and really became uncomfortable when we went out to eat or shop.

One instance illustrated this well. A few days after settling into our new hotel, we were in a local tourist mall. It was called the Tax Center, which I thought was not a very inviting name in English. Nevertheless, we enjoyed going through this multistory building full of local merchandise. On this one occasion, Jennifer simply could not lug Faith around any longer, so I was given the responsibility of keeping up with her.

Things started out well, with Faith in my arms while we looked at teacups, chess sets, dolls, and the world's largest inventory of chopsticks. Faith seemed content with me and I thought I would put her down to stand beside me and hold my hand. As soon as her little feet hit the floor she cried out like she was being tortured and ran off as fast as she could. I was amazed by how quick she was! Of course, I took off after her. She continued to scream out a string of words in Vietnamese with me in hot pursuit. Shopkeepers were appearing from a hundred stalls to see this pitiful little Vietnamese girl running in terror ahead of a clumsy American man. When I finally got my hands on her and wrestled her up into my arms, she was still screaming. A circle of Vietnamese women had formed around us. "They probably all know martial arts," I thought as I tried to smile and talk nice to my little one. With a poker face I said hello to the crowd and broke through the circle where I found Jennifer and the other two kids watching in amazement.

"Let's go back to the hotel," Jennifer suggested.

"Yeah."

\* \* \* \* \*

Although Faith seemed to be a little hesitant and afraid, her brother Joshua could get her to smile. He was kind to play with her and on one occasion he suffered a little embarrassment on her behalf. After we were transferred to Hanoi (where we were waiting for an appointment at the US Embassy), Joshua and I were in a crowded shopping district enjoying some guy time while Jennifer kept the girls back in the hotel. The two of us stood out like sore thumbs. Neither of us are tall, but somehow on the street in Hanoi we seemed enormous and glowing white.

Any attempt on our part to blend in was completely over when I noticed a vendor selling giant Hello Kitty Balloons. I knew that Grace and Faith would really enjoy these. After haggling with the balloon man, I added to our ridiculous look by having Joshua tote along two helium filled, jumbo size, Hello Kitties in our search for a cab. We barely fit in the back of a little Toyota, but once the balloons were safely in our hotel room it was worth it. I know this seems trivial, but for Faith, it might have been the first time she ever had someone come "home" and give her a present.

Faith was quiet during the daytime at the hotel or in the restaurant. She spent most of her waking time with her eyes fixed on Jennifer, a serious look on her little face with only an occasional smile. At night, she would wake up crying, sometimes screaming even. We would hold her a little and comfort her with something to drink. Her serious look would return and most of the time, she would go back to sleep. The routine probably sounds normal for anyone who has cared for a baby. However, Faith always seemed distant, even during our efforts to comfort or entertain her. It felt like she was unsure if she could trust us. This was the beginning of a long bonding process.

\* \* \* \* \*

After getting approval for Faith to emigrate to America from the US Embassy in Hanoi, we were ready to catch a plane for Jakarta. There was, however, one last drama that needed to play out. Faith had a visa to travel with us to America, but we were not going to America. We were headed back to Jakarta, Indonesia. No one had ever said we could not do this. It's just that no one had ever said we could, either, and we were afraid to ask. We did not have the time, money, or energy to fly our whole crew back to Jakarta via the United States.

At the Saigon Airport, I stood behind the yellow line with our little family waiting to approach the desk where our travel documents would be checked. I felt a little like a spy in a movie who was trying to smuggle something across the border. I had learned that by treaty, a Vietnamese citizen could enter Indonesia without a visa. This was good news, only the particular citizen in question was only two and she was traveling with a group of white folks who had been total strangers to her just weeks ago. A giant picture of Ho Chi Min himself glared down at us, adding to my discomfort as the control officer motioned us forward. He looked at each of our American passports, matching the passport photos with our faces. Then he picked Faith's green Vietnamese passport. He opened it, looked at her picture and then glanced up at her as she was held in Jennifer's arms. In that instant, the biggest smile I had seen broke out on her face. The officer smiled back, stamped her passport, and waved us on. "Praise God!" I thought. "We are on our way."

At the gate, we sat next to a group of swanky looking Vietnamese women who were headed to Singapore for a shopping trip. They smiled at us and then fixed their eyes on Faith. One woman spoke, "Why are you taking her?" Assuming she thought it strange for Americans to be headed out with a little Vietnamese girl, I explained we were adopting her. The woman replied, "Why would you do that? She's so ugly." She then stood up and walked off.

Although a little malnourished and scarred, little Faith was not ugly. The woman was not referring to her physical appearance. She just did not understand why we would place any value in the life of someone in Faith's situation. To this stranger, it made no sense to invest in a poor child when we could simply indulge ourselves in other things. We encountered this attitude a bit in Southeast Asia. Perhaps it exists in our own part of the world, too. Some people just cannot understand why you would accept an orphan. Thankfully, there are many people in Asia and everywhere who do want to help. And when they do, they are like our God in Heaven who is "Father to the fatherless... setting the lonely in families" (Ps. 68:5-6). It is a good thing that God has adopted us into his family instead of scorning our need, like so many hard-hearted people do in this world.

\* \* \* \* \*

We had a couple additional hurdles to jump after returning to Indonesia. We had hired an agent to help us through immigration at the Jakarta Airport, but were still apprehensive about bringing Faith into the country. She would be entering as a "tourist" until we got her an official visa as one of our dependents. Once again, however, our Sovereign God managed these small details. We entered through immigration just fine and we soon found ourselves riding home and entering our little house just like any other family back from vacation, except that we carried a sleepy little Vietnamese daughter in with us.

Once settled, we learned that Faith would need to get her official visa from an Indonesian embassy. That sounded simple at first, until it dawned on me that embassies are outside the country! The complication would have been insurmountable to me, but a friend at church came to our aid. This man worked for a large oil company and was familiar with how to get the correct visa from nearby Singapore. So, after breaking out the credit card again, Faith and I jetted across the Java Sea to the English-speaking city state.

It was a strange trip on at least two counts. First, although we traveled as father and daughter, Faith and I hardly knew each other. She was no trouble at all, but she sat looking warily at me with her serious expression. She maintained this demeanor the whole time, while we walked up and down Orchard Road. Singapore was true to its reputation as one of the cleanest cities in the world. It was refreshing to be outdoors there after the smog of Jakarta. Looking back, this was probably a good time for Faith and I to bond a little bit. At the time, however, we seemed like two strangers (one an adult and the other a child) thrown together in a strange city. It felt surreal.

Another unusual thing was the clandestine manner that we got her visa. I was green enough in that part of the world not to feel culpable at the time, but the circumstances were a bit, … mysterious. These were my instructions: "When you arrive in Singapore, go to the hotel restaurant and wait on a man in a suit. Give him your passports. Return to the restaurant at lunchtime the next day and the man will be there to give your passports back, Faith's with the proper visa." I followed the instructions. It worked and we were soon on our way back to Jakarta, where Faith entered as a foreign national resident of Indonesia.

## CHAPTER ELEVEN:
## POST-ADOPTION CHALLENGES

In April 2008, after Faith had been home with us for a couple of weeks, our four boys arrived from America. We had been apart for nearly 10 weeks. My brother Matthew had very kindly agreed to escort the kids across the world for us, but shortly before it was time to travel, he broke his foot. He was devastated, but obviously he could not make the long journey. Thankfully, Jennifer's sister Jill offered to bring them, enduring the 22-hour flight only to stay for a day before heading back.

It was great to see Andrew, Jacob, Simon Peter, and Elijah again. The weary travelers stumbled through the airport, looking exhausted, but they were a welcome sight. We had missed our kids so much. Although I pray the Lord will never ask us to split up our family like that again, the fruit of the separation was evident when the boys met Faith and she realized there were four more brothers in her new family!

The children quickly became attached to their youngest sister. It was especially easy for the boys. In fact, the five brothers seemed to have no trouble at all, accepting Faith instantly. It was almost as if she had been around all along. They played with her, talked with her, and even fussed with her a little, like kids do. It seemed very healthy. Grace also got along well with Faith from the very beginning. It did, however, take a little longer before they acted like sisters. I attribute this to two things. First, they are both girls and second, Grace had been the baby of the family until Faith came along. Of course, the two would both say they are best friends now.

Once we were settled in, it became apparent that Faith not only carried the scars of scabies on her little body. She was still carrying the nasty little critters, too. The whole family had to be treated. Each of us had to rub down head to toe with a medicinal ointment that was supposed to kill or repel the mites. In the morning, we had to shower and wash all the sheets in the house. Since we had to repeat this more than once, our poor house helper had the hardest time understanding this strange practice. She worked hard, and we nearly wore out our tiny little washing machine with seven sets of sheets being washed repeatedly. It was many weeks before we were scabies free.

As yucky as that was, I wish all adoption challenges could be treated with a tube of cream. It is normal, however, for adopted children and their families to struggle with bonding. One very positive thing I can say about the homestudy process we went through in Alabama is they made sure we were aware of this. We had to read several books on the topic and completed some writing assignments that were intended to help us think through possible problems with our accepting of Faith and her accepting us. Therefore, we anticipated that the adoption "process" would stretch beyond merely getting Faith home, and it is a good thing we did.

\* \* \* \* \*

Despite our best efforts, we simply could not complete Faith's citizenship application in Jakarta. I guess I should have known that to immigrate to America you do need to go there. So, by the first of June, we were once again purchasing plane tickets for three of us to travel to the United States. This was yet another unplanned expense to the tune of about $5,000 for plane tickets, not to mention expenses that would be incurred in America. It was at this time I realized I had stopped keeping track of the total cost of the adoption. It was easy to guess the amount was more than double the cost suggested by our agent in 2006. But as I said, I had stopped counting. We were going to finish no matter what.

We decided Jennifer, Joshua, and Faith should travel together to the States. They would stay about three weeks. We hoped, during that time, Faith could complete her citizenship process and then be eligible for a United States passport and other legal documents. Jennifer would also have an opportunity to take Faith to the International Adoption Clinic in Birmingham, Alabama for a battery of tests to see how she was doing. Once again, we divided our forces, but at least this time there was a parent in each bunch.

I was a wreck though. I always hate being without Jennifer. Seeing her and the two kids off at the airport was depressing. That same evening, I had been invited to the home of a family from our church and I would have to go without my dear wife. Rushing back in the heavy Jakarta traffic, I picked up the kids and we drove to our friend's house. We all piled out of the van (Andrew, Jacob, Simon Peter, Elijah, Grace, and me) and knocked on the door. When the lady of the house answered she seemed quite surprised. We had come on the wrong night! I have always known I could not survive without my better half.

\* \* \* \* \*

Jennifer was busy doing some more serious surviving of her own. She became incredibly airsick on her flight to the States and likely would have jumped out

113

of the plane had she been allowed to open the door. Thankfully, Joshua was there to help with Faith, so Jennifer could make it through. Once again, we could thank God for our oldest son's love and commitment to his family.

After arriving in North Carolina, Jennifer was picked up by her kind parents and taken to their Black Mountain home. It was while staying in Black Mountain that Jennifer began to feel the force of her biggest adoption challenge. She and Faith were experiencing serious bonding issues.

Reactive Attachment Disorder is a very real problem for children who are adopted. They struggle to fit into their new family emotionally and psychologically. All the little things that help a biological child bond with her parents, such as baby-cuddling, late night feeding, diaper changing, and so on, are not there for the toddler who is adopted at two. Sometimes children need therapy to overcome this and attach to their new family. We wanted to be sensitive to this with little Faith. Our strategy was to prepare for the worst and hope for the best. While there were moments when Faith struggled to know how she fit in, for the most part we can thank God that her adjustment has progressed steadily. Apart from her beautiful brown skin, she normally seems like any of our other kids.

Still, Jennifer and I each have a gloomy side to our adoption story which we think important to share. Adoption is not easy, but God's faithfulness in helping us through our struggles is proof that he can help others, too. As I shared already, my biggest difficulty was a lack of trust in the Lord for the finances. Jennifer's biggest struggle was difficulty bonding with Faith. While my struggle is evidence of unbelief, Jennifer's hardship had nothing to do with a lack of trust or obedience to God. It is just proof there is a powerful maternal attachment that naturally develops between a mom and her biological child which is not immediately present in the case of adoption.

I think it is easier for men to bond with adopted children because the process is not very different than with our biological children. We do not carry babies in our bodies, we do not go through the process of labor and delivery, we do not breastfeed or experience the hormonal changes a woman does in pregnancy and childbirth. For fathers, the bonding always takes place after the child has arrived. Bonding to an adopted daughter, while not exactly the same, is similar to the normal process. The adoptive mom, however, is missing those natural bonding elements. Obviously, there is nothing scientific about my analysis here. I am just sharing my experience and observations. I think it is important for two reasons.

First, I have noticed that one of the most common statements I hear from men as a reason not to adopt is, "I don't think I can love her like my own child." (They mean biological child.) Both nature and my own experience indicate this is not so. Men attach to adopted children in the same way they attach to biological children. The kids just appear in our lives and we begin to love and take care of them. Before we know it, there is an inseparable bond of love between us.

Second, as the old saying goes, "forewarned is forearmed." Adoptive moms need to know that adjusting to their new little one may not be a fairy tale experience. I suppose it can be, but it is best to prepare for a process that can be difficult and long, but totally worth it! Most people agree the very best things in this life do not come easy. Jennifer will tell you falling in love with an adopted child is one of the greatest joys in life, but there is more process involved than many people expect.

\* \* \* \* \*

When we were in Vietnam, Faith quickly attached herself to Jennifer. We had been taught this was likely to happen. At first, an adopted child will typically attach to just one other person. This is considered good, so I was not discouraged to see that Faith had chosen Jennifer to be her "comfort and safety" person. However, as the weeks went on and we returned to our home, the demands Faith placed on Jennifer's attention became overwhelming. It was especially troublesome at night. Faith would wake up screaming and totally inconsolable. Her emotions were strange. She would be crying but did not seem sad or scared. It was like something was bothering her emotionally, but she did not know how to process it. She would break into sweats that would leave her totally sopping wet and there was nothing we could do to calm her down.

While Jennifer was away in North Carolina, the nighttime screaming fits continued and would wake up everyone in the house. It was a frustrating time that really strained the bonding between Jennifer and Faith. Some of this was simply because it is hard to handle difficulty when you are sleep deprived and part of it was because Faith would not respond positively to the kind of care our biological children had received from their mom. The essential point was that Jennifer and Faith were not enjoying the kind of mother and daughter relationship we had envisioned.

It is not without hesitation and a little embarrassment that we share this detail. Jennifer will tell you she remembers reading about adoptive moms who had trouble bonding with their adopted children and thinking "that will never be a struggle for me." So why put this sensitive detail in print? Because we want to do all we can to equip other families who are thinking of adopting. We want them to be ready for what might lay ahead as a means of helping ensure their success. We also have some encouragement along with a bit of advice.

The encouragement is that things do get better. Those screaming, sweaty nights are over for us now. Faith is happy and comfortable in her family. Today, we rarely ever think about bonding or attachment issues, unless it is to celebrate how good things feel. Jennifer and Faith have made significant progress with bonding and appear knit together emotionally just as any other mother and daughter would be. Our progress has been in a positive direction. It is a reminder that hard times and struggles do not mean hopeless times. Things can and (especially with our Lord's help) do get better!

Our advice is to seek out all the help you can. There are some obvious advantages to adopting an Asian daughter while living in Asia. For example, we have never felt the need to attend an Asian festival here in the states in order to better understand Faith's cultural history. Our family has been deeply immersed in Asian culture. However, if we had lived in America when we adopted Faith, we would have access to more adoption counseling resources, such as those offered by the International Adoption Clinic in Birmingham, Alabama. We would have made use of those options. Our advice to potential and new adoptive parents is that they should not be shy about getting professional help. Adopting is a wonderful, awesome, worthwhile challenge. But it is a challenge. The best things in this world are not easy. Adoption is not easy. There is no shame in admitting it and getting all the assistance you can for the sake of your child, not to mention your own mental, emotional, and spiritual health.

\* \* \* \* \*

On June 6, 2008 Ngo Thi Xuan Mai, formally became Faith Hadassah St. John, a citizen of the United States of America. She received a letter from the president along with a certificate of citizenship. In this way, she joined the millions of other people who have found America to be a welcoming culture full of opportunity for the future. Nevertheless, our little Vietnamese-American girl was soon on a plane headed back to Jakarta, Indonesia where her adoptive family had made their home.

## CHAPTER TWELVE:
## CONCLUSION (FOR NOW)

With her American citizenship in hand, Faith returned to our home in Jakarta and settled into a routine like that of American expatriate kids all over the world. She played baby dolls with her sister, enjoyed games with her brothers, slept well, ate well, and made friends. We worked hard to maintain a healthy and honest approach, making the fact she is the only Asian and adopted child in our family an example of how God has made each one of us special in some way.

We lived and worked in Indonesia for four years before moving back to the United States. I spent an impromptu sabbatical year doing post-graduate work at Southeastern Seminary before moving out to Pueblo, Colorado to serve as pastor at Calvary Church. After a couple of years with the folks there, we were ready to relocate to my hometown of Knoxville, Tennessee. We are thankful to have settled near our extended family here and I am involved in a growing Christian ministry for homeschool families.

Kids grow fast. I know it sounds cliché, but it is true. Joshua and Andrew have both married and we now have three beautiful grandchildren. Jacob is off at school with an interest in missions. Simon is in college studying Chemical engineering. Jennifer, the kids still at home, and I continue to stumble along, attempting to do something good for the needy children of this world. Not too long ago, we became foster parents and had two little foster kids living with us. It was another wild ride and frankly, it hurt a lot. However, I hope the story of Faith's adoption demonstrates that the best things in life do not come easy. They are, nevertheless, the best things. And following in the footsteps of our Lord who set aside his glory and majesty to help spiritual orphans like all of us is something we never need to second guess or apologize for, no matter how it goes. The Lord tells us that serving the needy is how we have "pure religion."

Recently, Jennifer, the kids, and I began praying and actively pursuing another adoption. Like our other adventures, I am sure there will be some tough patches, but our God is ever faithful, and we are ready to move ahead. Among other plans, we will always use the proceeds from this book to support adoption, either in our home or someone else's.

I hope the Lord is speaking to you as you think about the needs of orphans. Perhaps you have always wanted to adopt but thought you couldn't because of some limitation in your life. It seems to me that if our family could adopt with the few resources we had and all the upheaval we experienced, then anybody who is open to the Lord's leading can do it! Or maybe you know a couple wanting to adopt, but they need assistance. God might be calling you to help them rescue an orphan from an uncertain future by supporting them financially or in some other way. Let's be brave for our Lord and reach out to the needy little ones of this earth. As John Piper has said, "As long as there is a Christian Church in the world, there should be no orphans!"

May our King Jesus get all the glory for everything He has done! Anything good that has happened to our family is from Him! We own the responsibility for all the mistakes and failures. Also, special thanks to Faith Hadassah St. John, the girl who was in the picture but now has a place in our hearts.

# BIBLIOGRAPHY

Champnella, Cindy. 2004. *The Waiting Child: How the Faith and Love of One Orphan Saved the Life of Another.* Reprint edition. New York: St. Martin's Griffin.

John Piper. 2003. *Don't Waste Your Life.* Wheaton: Crossway.

"The KIM Foundation International: Healing Children of War." 2018. http://www.kimfoundation.com.

# ABOUT THE AUTHOR

Stephen St. John has served as a pastor, missionary, and educator. Along with his wife and seven children, Stephen has lived and worked in the United States, Madagascar, and Indonesia.

Stephen is a graduate of Covenant College and Covenant Theological Seminary.

Stephen enjoys running, reading, spending time with his family, and taking long walks with his beloved wife Jennifer.

Correspondence with Stephen can be sent to: throughfaithbook@gmail.com

Made in the USA
Columbia, SC
07 March 2025

54827279R00081